The Invisible Empire

The Invisible Empire
The Ku Klux Klan Impact on History

by William Loren Katz

Open Hand Publishing Inc.
Washington, DC

Open Hand Publishing Inc.
210 Seventh Street, SE, Suite A24
Washington, DC
(202) 659-9250

Library of Congress
Catalog Card Number: 86-62297

ISBN: 0-940880-15-6

Illustrations and photographs are from the William Loren Katz Collection, New York City

Printed in the United States of America

91 90 89 88 87 86   7 6 5 4 3 2 1

DEDICATION

"The method of force which hides itself in secrecy is a method as old as humanity. The kind of thing that men are afraid or ashamed to do openly, and by day, they accomplish secretly, masked, and at night. . . . [This method] need hesitate at no outrage or maiming or murder, it shields itself in the mob mind and then throws over all a veil of darkness which becomes glamour."
—W.E.B. DuBois, *Black Reconstruction* (1935), pp. 677-678.

This volume is dedicated to those little known women and men, black, red or white, who challenged the "veil of darkness."

The unknown Black woman in 1868 who began the resistance with a broom; the anonymous white North Carolinian who defied the Klan by giving land to his former slaves; White Robert Flournoy of Mississippi who fought by building schools and Black Samuel Allen who fought by teaching in them; Major Lewis Merrill, whose investigations in the 1870s repesented the best his race, his North, and his Federal government could give.

Ida B. Wells, who in Memphis, Tennessee in 1892 launched the first crusade against lynchings, and ex-slave George H. White, Congressman from North Carolina, who in 1900 introduced the first anti-lynching bill.

Walter White and William Allen White in the 1920s; the Scottsboro Mothers, William Anderson and Angelo Herndon in the 1930s; Stetson Kennedy and Harry Moore in the 1940s; the Lumbee Indians and Robert Williams — all of Robeson County, North Carolina in the 1950s; Councilman Ben Davis and William Patterson who kept at it from the 1930s to 1950s.

And the martyrs of the 1960s symbolized by James Chaney, Andrew Goodman, Michael Schwerner.

And to those who remind us the fight still goes on. . .Julian Bond, Morris Dees, Ann Braden, Eddie Carthan and Reverend James Lowrey.

TABLE OF CONTENTS

PREFACE

THIS PROJECT GREW OUT OF MY belief that schools and colleges do not offer what students need to know about the Ku Klux Klan. My concern began as a student at Syracuse University in 1950 when a course on *The Civil War and Reconstruction* introduced me to what purported to be a history of The Invisible Empire. The professor's bigotry in defense of the hooded order permeated his lectures and "Justify the actions of the Ku Klux Klan" was a final examination assignment.

Although I had researched the KKK previously, in the 1970s I began a book on the subject, signed a contract with a major publisher, and completed a manuscript by 1981. Then a mean, Klan-like spirit began to dog its trail to the printer.

The company Vice President who served as editor exploded that my depiction of the early Klan was "blatantly prejudiced." Her letter insisted that while she "does not justify the KKK, there is an historical basis for the anger." After again insisting "No one is apologizing for the KKK," she relied on the Klan's own justification—that Blacks after slavery "were running rampant." She referred me to a particular volume on the subject. This book was one the National Education Association had called "appalling" because it contains "gross stereotypes about blacks," and because it "romanticizes and condones . . . the terrorist nature of the first Klan."

My arguments failed to persuade her, and my contract was terminated. It was New York in 1981, but it felt like Syracuse University in 1950. Most incredibly, this exchange took place after tumultuous decades of Civil Rights activities had created new Federal legislation, and scholars had begun to reveal a more accurate US racial history.

I began to search for another home for my Klan manuscript but encountered one publisher's rejection notice after another. Only the first openly challenged my views on the Klan; others cited an old publishers'

1

creed that potential sales are pivotal in deciding if a book deserves publication. This "bottom line" guessing creates a gulf between information the public needs and a publisher's response to such needs.

In researching, writing—and seeking a publisher for—this book, I have arrived at several conclusions I would like to share with readers. First, an accurate study of Klan history has value precisely because it casts light on some crucial intellectual distortions that shore up ingrained racism. I believe this history has a lot to teach Americans, young people in particular, and not least of all, friends and members of The Invisible Empire.

Second, stories of dogged resistance by targets of the Klan constitute a little known aspect of our national heritage, and deserve a wider audience. In emphasizing the Klan's capabilities for intimidation and violence, many writers have neglected instances when intrepid defiance halted Klan aggression.

Third, few citizens realize that at times the intensity of Klan terrorism has changed the history and altered the morality of states and whole regions. Fourth, even fewer know that this was possible because society's leading figures and officials have encouraged, conspired with or relied on the hooded order. Last, of all modern countries, only U.S. citizens have paid for an independent armed strike force for racial injustice for more than a century. If the past is a guide, violent Klansmen can be counted on to burst sporadically upon an uncertain future.

It is a daring act of faith, seasoned with a dash of uncommon courage, for my editor, Anna Rodieck, to place tiny Open Hand's resources behind this project. Working with those at Open Hand who share my view of the subject's significance has been a rewarding experience. Considerably expanded and altered, this battle-scarred manuscript has finally been baptised with printer's ink.

I have tried to contain, since no one can avoid, the passions this subject stirs in human beings. I have also tried to shape this story into a form so logical and language so clear that students who don't enjoy reading history and adults who have little time for it—and even Klan members—will want to find out what happens.

If this book fills that tall order, it can serve a useful purpose.

William Loren Katz

Birth of an
Invisible Empire:
1866 to 1875

1

A WEIRD POTENCY
IN THE VERY NAME

IT BEGAN INNOCENTLY ENOUGH. SIX YOUNG men in sleepy, Pulaski, Tennessee, found life after the Civil War dull and dreary. As Confederate soldiers, they lived through the thrills of charging up and down hills, shooting and being shot at, facing cannon fire and cavalry attacks. But in May, 1866, the war had been over for a year and they thirsted for adventure, excitement and some rollicking fun.

They decided to form a club.

So John Lester, James Crowe, John Kennedy, Richard Reed, Frank McCord and Calvin Jones met one night in the late Spring to form a club. Their meeting place was also innocent—the office of Calvin Jones' father, Judge Thomas L. Jones.

Committees were picked to select a good club name and some special ceremonies. The names chosen—The Merry Six or the Pulaski Social Club—were considered poor. No, members agreed, the name must be attractive, one that would stir mystery and excite interest.

The six young men came from families with a good education. They knew about Greek letter fraternities in colleges, and their favorite was *Kuklos Adelphon*. In Greek, *kyklos* means a circle of friends. That was it. Ku-Klux, they called themselves, and added Klan for more zip. They figured "Ku Klux Klan" would make people sit up and take notice, and they were right. Some years later John Lester wrote down his recollections of those early days: "There was a weird potency in the very name Ku Klux Klan."

One wonders what might have happened if they had chosen The Merry Six or the Pulaski Social Club.

Out to the public the six went to recruit new members. They decided to disguise their identities. "Each member," Lester wrote, "provided himself with the following outfit: a white mask for the face, with orifices for the eyes and nose; a tall, fantastic cardboard hat, so constructed as to increase the wearer's apparent height; a gown, or robe, of sufficient length to cover the

7

entire person." No particular color or material was set so members chose colorful costumes that Lester believed were "hideous and fantastic" and "most flashy."

To keep people from recognizing their voices, the masked young men communicated by blowing on children's whistles. In their strange outfits and talking by whistling, the Klansmen began attending fairs and social gatherings. They began to attract other bored young men to their adventures.

Early Klan outfits, 1868.

"To harmonize with the name," Lester wrote, the club selected strange rituals. The officers were a Grand Cyclops (President), Grand Magi (Vice President), Grand Turk (Marshal), and Grand Exchequer (Treasurer). Members were called "Ghouls," met in a "Den" that was guarded by two "Lictors."

To initiate new members, the Klan found a dreary house in the country surrounded by gaunt trees that created a weird feeling. Candidates were blindfolded, led into a damp cellar and over obstacles. Finally, they were brought before the Grand Cyclops and asked silly, complicated or senseless questions.

At the end, the blindfold was torn away and the new recruit, wearing donkey's ears, faced a large mirror. Klansmen burst into laughter and welcomed the startled new member. Then, he was sworn to "absolute secrecy" about the club, its rituals and its members.

That was the birth of the dreaded Ku Klux Klan—little whistles and strange costumes, mirrors and donkey's ears, silly tricks, giggles and laughter.

The club caught on and new members flocked in. The young men of Pulaski found an amusement to fill their lives. So far no one had suggested riding out at night to whip or murder anyone. No one suggested that terrifying neighbors, Blacks or Yankees was either a good idea or any fun. No one insisted that the White race needed saving and the Ku Klux Klan was the club to do it.

That soon changed.

Den No. 2 formed across the state line in Athens, Alabama. Its members became infuriated by a new school set up to educate Black children. The white teachers, said one member of the Athens Klan, were "treating their students as human beings." That would not do, decided the Athens Den.

The first action taken by the Den was to seize a Black student who had been "too friendly with his teacher." Taken out in the middle of the night, the student was thrown into an icy brook. This was no prank that everyone enjoyed, but a painful lesson in race relations, and directed at an innocent student. The laughter had a mean-spirited cutting edge.

This Den adopted the aim of "maintaining white supremacy." Soon Klans throughout the 11 states of the Old Confederacy united behind this goal. The strange costumes, disguises and the secrecy would be used to further that aim—to force Black people into ignorance and a new slavery—and hand Whites the reins of southern power. From the Mason-Dixon line to the Rio Grande border, the Ku Klux Klan became dedicated to enforcing racial inequality by intimidation and violence.

In April, 1868, Frank McCord was editor of the Pulaski *Citizen*. He printed a letter from another of the original six members. It complained about the Ku Klux Klan. "The simple object of the original Ku-Kluxes," the letter said, had become "so perverted. Better the Ku Klux had never been heard of."

The letter was unsigned. Now even this founder was afraid of the secret order he had helped create.

2

ROOTS OF
KLAN THINKING

A BELIEF IN WHITE SUPREMACY HAS powered the Ku Klux Klan since its early days in the South. But the secret order did not invent the idea. It was carried across the Atlantic and planted in the soil of the New World by the first European explorers to these shores. It took root when Europeans said they had a right to enslave Native Americans and seize their lands. Soon a brisk slave trade kidnapped Africans in their homeland for the slave markets of the New World, and this too was justified by the creed of White supremacy.

By the time the Founding Fathers signed the Declaration of Independence and the U.S. Constitution, bondage was an accepted part of American life. Northerners and southerners held slaves, and both sought to justify their profitable holdings in human bondage. Few—except for its victims—dared challenge a system so useful, profitable and beneficial.

Men invented both simple and complicated fantasies to explain and justify their system. The key claim was that Europeans were "superior" (and Africans "inferior") and this entitled Whites to enslave Blacks. This theory was able to explain in exactly what ways Africans were inferior to Europeans—they were not Christian, not White and not European. This meant that White people saw them as "not civilized."

From school, pulpit and newspaper, this version of life was carefully imparted to young and old. Those who questioned or debated the fantasy were insulted, threatened, driven away and sometimes slain. On slavery, insisted the slave masters who ruled the South, the region would speak with one sure voice.

Slavery benefited a few owners, and led to an arrangement that determined the lives of the South's eight million other Whites. The theory of White supremacy insisted that what mattered was a white skin, and it promised the lowliest Whites privileges no Black person had. These Whites could say, feel and act superior.

GANG OF 25 SEA ISLAND
COTTON AND RICE NEGROES,
By LOUIS D. DE SAUSSURE.

On *THURSDAY* the 25th Sept., 1852, at 11 o'clock, **A.M.**, will be sold at RYAN'S MART, in Chalmers Street, in the City of Charleston,

A prime gang of 25 Negroes, accustomed to the culture of Sea Island Cotton and Rice.

CONDITIONS. — One-half Cash, balance by Bond, bearing interest from day of sale, payable in one and two years, to be secured by a mortgage of the negroes and approved personal security. Purchasers to pay for papers.

No.	Age.	Capacity.	No.	Age.	Capacity.
1 Aleck,	33	Carpenter.	16 Hannah,	60	Cook.
2 Mary Ann,	31	Field hand, prime.	17 Cudjoe,	22	Prime field hand.
3—3 Louisa,	10		3—18 Nancy,	20	Prime field hand, sister of Cudjoe.
4 Abram,	25	Prime field hand.			
5 Judy,	24	Prime field hand.	19 Hannah,	34	Prime field hand.
6 Carolina,	5		20 James,	13	Slight defect in knee from a broken leg.
7 Simon,	1½		21 Richard,	9	
5—8 Daphne, infant.			22 Thomas,	6	
			5—23 John,	3	
9 Daniel,	45	Field hand, not prime.			
10 Phillis,	32	Field hand.	1—24 Squash,	40	Prime field hand.
11 Will,	9				
12 Daniel,	6		1—25 Thomas,	28	Prime field hand.
13 Margaret,	4				
14 Delia	2				
7—15 Hannah,	2 months.				

"Courtesy Pioneer Historical Society"

Charleston, South Carolina poster in 1852 tells the story of slavery in simple statistics and names.

But time after time poor Whites found that they could not compete with slave labor, and their wages remained miserably low. They had few opportunities for advancement, and no chance for education. They lived on the hope that someday they might become rich enough to own slaves. This too was a myth. White supremacy, then, tied poor Whites to a system that held everyone down except slave masters.

The North which slowly eliminated slavery as unprofitable, still continued to believe in White supremacy—and continued to supply ships and supplies for slave-hunters who sailed to Africa. New England continued to produce slavery's whips and chains for southern masters and overseers. Boston and New York were key trading ports for the lucrative southern market based on human bondage.

The Civil War, then, pitted armies against one another that believed in their own White supremacy. But during the long conflict, these beliefs took a beating. Many "inferiors" fled their "superiors" and sought an opportunity to take up arms against their former masters. At first, Whites, including Abraham Lincoln, scoffed at the notion that Black men could do any serious fighting against Whites. But in time the laughter stopped and 226,000 ex-slaves joined the Union Army and Navy. They fought bravely and 18 Black men earned Congressional Medals of Honor in combat against their former masters.

But old ideas die hard, especially if they benefit people, and White superiority still had a lot of fuel left to burn. After four bloody years, the South lost its effort to become an independent Confederacy, and lost its slaves. It suffered hundreds of thousands killed and wounded, and many of its towns, cities and huge plantations lay in ruins.

Peace left Confederate veterans and wealthy southern planters embittered. They hated Yankees, hated losing their valuable free labor and hated the very idea of ex-slaves being at liberty. Most sputtered in fury that they would never in any way treat former slaves as their equals.

The rules of bondage had refused Blacks basic rights to education or advancement. To learn to read or write was a crime. But before the war was over thousands of Black women, men and children had learned their ABC's. Once free many began building homes, schools and churches. They looked forward to a free life that provided them the

At the time of the Battle of Gettysburg in 1863, Whites in New York City set fire to a Black orphanage on Fifth Avenue and 42nd Street.

same opportunities for education, good jobs, and land that White people had always enjoyed.

This fond hope collided with the fantasies spun to justify slavery. These myths did not quickly retreat or vanish because President Lincoln announced "a new birth of freedom." Led by former slave owners, many southern Whites refused to accept the end of bondage, and clinging to their notions of superiority, most rejected any ideas of Black freedom or equality.

At the war's end, those men with the greatest stake in the Confederacy, slavery and White supremacy remained in charge of their state and local governments. As the voice of power and privilege in the South, they were prepared to put Black freedom to a fiery test. Their unyielding efforts to prevent their former slaves from achieving the promise of liberty shaped southern history and life for more than a hundred years. It would also have a profound impact on US history.

Unaware of the awesome powers arrayed against them, ex-slaves eagerly rushed from the plantations seeking a new life. They knew that they were free and meant to try it out. Many began to search for loved ones separated from them by slave auctions and sales. Some began to create families, find new jobs and build homes and communities. Each step of the way the ex-slaves encountered a White society determined to drive them back toward the chains the Civil War had forever smashed.

The loud arguments over the rights of ex-slaves reached from the smallest communities in the land to the White House. When Abraham Lincoln was assassinated, Andrew Johnson became President. While Lincoln, like other Whites of his time, doubted whether the two races were

A Civil War veteran.

equal, he was open-minded and flexible. Johnson was bigoted and inflexible, jealous of rich Whites, angry at Blacks.

As a poor, uneducated, White apprentice, he had learned the lessons of White supremacy well. When White mobs attacked Black families in Memphis and New Orleans in 1866, President Johnson blamed the Black victims. When a Black delegation asked him to grant their people voting rights, he said this would cause a racial war. Though he suggested that Black people look to him as "a Moses" to lead them, Johnson thought peace in the United States required the protection of White privileges, not Black rights.

With President Andrew Johnson encouraging former southerners who had led the rebellion to control Black citizens, and Congress determined to prevent this, the country headed toward inevitable conflict. Leading the Congressional opposition to President Johnson were Senator Charles Sumner and Representative Thaddeus Stevens. They had championed the cause of anti-slavery and now believed freedom depended upon Confederate leaders being denied office and Black people receiving equal rights and perhaps land. Otherwise, they warned, victories won on bloody battlefields would disappear and former slaves would again fall under the whips of their old masters.

Even as President Johnson urged Black southerners to remain calm, his own investigator, Carl Schurz, reported to him on unchanging White attitudes. Schurz's report to Johnson included a statement from Colonel Samuel Thomas, in charge of Federal relief efforts in Mississippi and Louisiana:

> Wherever I go—the street, the shop, the house, the hotel, or the steamboat—I hear people talk in such a way as to indicate that they are yet unable to conceive of the negro as possessing any rights at all. . . . The people boast that when they get freedom affairs in their own hands, to use their own classic expression, "the niggers will catch hell."
>
> The reason for all this is simple and manifest. The whites esteem the blacks their property by natural right, and however much they may admit that the individual relations of masters and slaves have been destroyed by the war and by the President's emancipation proclamation, they still have an ingrained feeling that the blacks at large belong to the whites at large. . . .

This "ingrained feeling" of racial superiority had to be seriously challenged if the South was to remain at peace. Without that strong challenge, White men would feel righteous in saddling their horses and riding out to kill Black people for simply exercising their freedom. Unless it was strongly attacked and undermined, Whites would feel White supremacy was still a just cause.

As Black people tried out their new liberty to do what they wanted, fearful Whites thought a violent revolution was about to explode in their

Civil War casualties, 1865. (Harper's Weekly)

midst. Those who believed that Africans were best off under White masters, now claimed that this freedom would threaten White lives, perhaps destroy society itself. A southern doctor rushed into a US Army outpost convinced that Black people planned "an outbreak at any moment." His only proof: a Black woman of 18 who had been his slave once and still worked for him. . .refused to accept a whipping.

The White South included many people who thought that any instance of Black liberty spelled terrible trouble. Worse, they felt they were justified in confronting any possible threat with armed and massive violence.

If proof was needed that the old Confederacy had not died on the battlefields of the Civil War, it came from the first southern election results after the war. Elected to Congress in 1866 were 58 Confederate Congressmen, 9 Confederate Generals and Admirals, 6 Confederate Cabinet members and the Vice President of the Confederacy, Alexander H. Stephens. In this election, Blacks could not vote and neither could most Whites.

This victory by men who had just led the country into four years of

17

rebellion brought a swift reaction in the North. Congress refused to seat these ex-Confederates, and they were sent home while Congress debated how to "reconstruct" the South. In Mississippi, one planter said:

> We showed our hand too soon. We ought to have waited until the troops were withdrawn, and our representatives admitted to Congress. Then we could have had everything our way.

3

THE DREAM
OF RECONSTRUCTION

WHILE CONGRESS AND THE PRESIDENT WRANGLED over the best way to reconstruct the 11 seceded states, forces committed to White supremacy assembled, mounted their horses and swept across the southland. They chose two paths of action, one violently illegal, the other barely legal, both approaches part of a carefully-drawn conspiracy.

They targeted ex-slaves, often former Union soldiers, who had become leaders in their communities. Often the most successful and ambitious Black farmers or community figures—or their family members—were ambushed on lonely country roads. At about the same time, White legislators in each of the former Confederate states passed "Black Codes" to replace the old "Slave Codes." Little changed.

Mississippi simply replaced the word "slave" in its old laws with "Black" for the new codes governing free people. Everywhere in the South "Black Codes" required that ex-slaves be employed by a White person and could not change jobs without a White's permission. Unemployed Blacks were arrested for "vagrancy" and then assigned work without pay. Black children without parents were rounded up and used as forced labor. As in bondage, Blacks had to work and Whites were their legal, all-powerful employers.

The new freedom began to look more and more like the old slavery. Blacks still could not vote, hold office or speak up to a White person. States did not establish schools for ex-slaves, and those adults or children who pursued an education were viewed as dangerous to White society.

The dreaded slave patrols returned to the countryside. In the service of wealthy planters, poor whites were again armed and sent out to terrorize Blacks into accepting a lowly status. These "patrollers" also persecuted Whites who had opposed secession or had favored the North during the war. The harassment and assassination of "disloyal"

White southerners increasingly included those who thought ex-slaves deserved an equal chance to land, decent jobs and education.

Under the guise of enforcing law, patrollers ran their own vigilante system. U.S. General Charles Howard reported that they gave "the color of law to their violent, unjust and inhuman acts." The actions of patrollers set the stage for riders of The Invisible Empire.

Northerners hoped in vain that the decisive defeat of the Confederacy and slavery had changed hearts and minds in the South. But each day

After slavery, armed slave patrols returned to the countryside, stopping and examining passes required of all Black people. New Orleans, Louisiana.

the news was discouraging. The new laws and the old violence against Blacks demonstrated that White supremacy not only failed to accept defeat, but was roaring back invigorated, armed and thirsting for battle.

By 1866, Whites had declared war against newly-freed slaves in widely scattered regions of the South and received important encouragement. When Whites rioted against Blacks in Memphis, Tennessee, in the Spring, 1866, killing 46 and wounding another 80, one newspaper rejoiced "Thank heaven the White race are once more rulers of Memphis." A few months later, the Mayor of New Orleans and his police led a White mob that killed 34 and wounded 200 Black people. This murderous assault on innocent citizens was also trumpeted as a victory for "White people."

The mounting anti-Black violence and the Black Codes sounded an alarm in the North. The Republican Party feared they announced a broad challenge to its power over the defeated Confederacy. Parents who had lost sons defeating the Confederacy petitioned their Congressmen to punish and regulate a White South that did not accept the verdict of the battlefield.

As they poised to act, they were blocked by President Johnson who sought compromise with leaders of the old Confederacy. They sharpened their weapons for a massive constitutional clash. Radical Republican Congressmen moved dramatically to take charge of reconstruction. They charged the President with using powers that were not his, and allowing defeated traitors to ride back into power.

Congress and President entered upon an historic collision course that ended with the impeachment of President Johnson, and Congress ruling the defeated South. It meant that for up to a decade in the South, a U.S. Army of occupation would stand as the single force preserving the peace, restoring order and protecting citizenship and property rights.

In any southern election, Republicans needed more votes than they had in the South. They solved this problem by prohibiting ex-Confederates from voting and granting the franchise to former slaves and poor Whites who had never voted. For the next decade, a large Black vote upheld Republican party rule in the South. By sweeping key states of the South, Black voters insured the Republicans would remain the leading party in national elections.

Ironically, this Republican party that became dependent upon the votes of poor Black and White southerners, was led by the North's richest industrialists and financial tycoons. An alliance between economic classes so diverse could not last.

But in the years that it did, it created within the heart of the South a unique model for racial relations in the United States. To insure that President Johnson could not interfere with its plans, Congress passed the 14th and 15th Amendments establishing Blacks voting rights. They were ratified by a majority of the states.

Andrew Johnson could not stop Constitutional Amendments and he was not nominated to run for the White House, but he still possessed

Election scene, Washington, DC. June 3, 1867

vast Presidential powers. He leaped into the fray, vetoing Congressional laws, appointing southern military commanders and officials imbued with his viewpoint, and removing those who disagreed. He pardoned ex-Confederate leaders and returned confiscated plantations to them—sometimes having the Army tearing lands away from hard-working ex-slaves who had settled them.

In the midst of the confrontation in Washington, Southern Blacks were also on the move. Working for their former masters, they felt, seemed too much like a ticket back to slavery, so they struck out on their own. They bought land or sought employment for their skills in town. They insisted that only by having the political rights of citizens could they protect their families' liberties and gain some land. Each Black step forward met with a violent and often armed resistance.

This White force would soon be commanded in battle under the name of The Invisible Empire or The Knights of the Ku Klux Klan. The time was set for its arrival on the scene as the cutting edge of White supremacy diehards in the South.

$$* \quad * \quad * \quad * \quad *$$

There are rare moments in history when a fateful clash of people results in a new arrangement of society. The Spring of 1867 witnessed such an explosive moment. Congress ordered new constitutional conventions in ten southern states, and enfranchised the White and Black voters who selected the delegates. To enforce its order, it dispatched Federal troops to protect the Black and White voters and delegates.

The Black and White delegates, most of whom had not previously participated in a democratic process, talked about equal justice. As Federal bayonets guarded their deliberations, former slaves, former masters, and poor Whites wrote the first democratic constitutions their states had ever known. Though it was not their primary purpose, their very presence also initiated a uniquely different tradition in the history of racial relations in the United States.

These state conventions advanced democracy on a broad front. Representative government gained in the South when all adult males whether they owned property or not were granted the right to vote.

23

In Charleston, South Carolina, 1865, Black teachers established a school in a room that had previously been used to auction slaves.

Previously, only the minority of men who owned property were voters. Appointed government offices, often filled by friends of the wealthy who voted, were made part of the election process.

The state constitutional convention's greatest contribution to its people was the creation of the South's first public school system. In an age that viewed education as the magic gateway to financial, cultural and social success, schools were opened to Black and White alike.

The Conventions also increased rights for women and made the tax burden easier for the poor, heavier for the rich. Money was appropriated to improve roads, bridges, government buildings, insane asylums, hospitals and prisons. The poor could no longer be whipped or thrown in jail for debt or executed for minor crimes.

These conventions brought the promise of America to people who had long been denied its benefits—and tried to make sure that race or wealth did not determine the rights of citizenship.

At the moment a new order was being formulated by southern men meeting in democratic conventions, the Ku Klux Klan emerged as its most serious armed challenge. If White supremacy was to survive, reasoned its champions, then Blacks must not be permitted to prove they can make intelligent use of political or economic power. Black landowners and successful businessmen must be ruined, Black politicians undermined, driven off or killed.

Those who organized hundreds of thousands of mounted troops into the Ku Klux Klan also defined its terrorist aims with precision. If Whites were allowed to work and vote alongside Blacks, the White supremacy structure would collapse forever. In a land that profitted from a labor force divided by skin color, Black and White must not unite. At any cost in pain and death, Black labor power must be chained to White mastery.

Further, there must be no outside interference with this plan. Whites from the South or North who aided Blacks had to be driven off, intimidated or slain. The US government had to be persuaded that it was a useless waste of energy and tax money to oppose the will and might of White supremacy.

These became the goals of The Invisible Empire, the Ku Klux Klan. While the President of the United States and Congress debated who would run reconstruction in the South, the secret order transformed itself into a massive terrorist strike force. Then it tried to direct southern reconstruction from the barrel of a gun, the end of a lynch rope and a lighted torch.

In the Spring of 1867, the Pulaski Den summoned a meeting of key Klans at the big Maxwell House Hotel, in Nashville, Tennessee. Little is known about this first unity meeting of southern Klan forces, for no notes were kept. Attending were former high ranking officers of the Confederate armed forces, wealthy southern landowners and businessmen. It is not known if General Nathan Bedford Forrest, who soon became the Klan's Grand Wizard, was present. Soon after the meeting ended, he took over administration of the organization.

Delegates adopted a table of organization and chain of command reminiscent of a military unit. Klan mumbo-jumbo coded the months of the year with names such as Dismal and Dark, and the days of the week were named after colors. Since secrecy was crucial, Klan goals were not identified. Since the aims were illegal and well known to all attending, it was neither necessary nor wise to put them on paper. Even the Ku Klux Klan name remained secret for a year.

A *Prescript* restricted membership to young men 18 years of age or older, recommended by a member. Women were not admitted, for mayhem and violence were considered "man's work." Recruits were required to swear an oath of secrecy—under threat of death—about all Klan matters and members.

In 1868, a revised *Prescript* appeared that included ten questions. Klan recruits were asked if they had ever served in the US Army, organizations that supported the Republican party, or if they believed in racial

May 2, 1866. Riot in Memphis, Tennessee.

equality. A "yes" answer to any question would keep one from enrolling.

Klan propaganda generously portrayed itself as "an institution of Chivalry, Humanity, Mercy and Patriotism." They said they were citizens "noble in sentiment, generous in manhood and patriotic in purpose" seeking to "protect the weak, the innocent and the defenseless" from "the lawless, the violent and the brutal."

The Invisible Empire became the first criminal organization in U.S. history to claim it was kind and good, and that its victims were really the violent ones. Until the rise of Hitler's stormtroopers more than a half century later, no armed force would carry out such systematic attacks on helpless civilian populations, and with such deadly effectiveness. Both Nazis and Klansmen marched into battle under the banner of a "superior race."

Members were generally between 18 and 35, unmarried and from rich and middle-class families. Poor Whites were enrolled as members but the reins of Klan power were tightly held by those wealthy land-owners and businessmen who benefited most by terrorizing Black labor into a new degrading slavery.

Klansmen preferred to portray themselves as "southern patriots" who gallantly championed the South's "lost cause" and the Confederate flag. From its beginnings, the Klan nostalgically identified with and tried to revive an era and system that had died.

For many members, joining a secret armed network also spoke to deep psychological needs. For those who felt they lacked control over their lives, it offered life and death power over others. It promised all members a claim of superiority over anyone who was Black. It also brought the less successful shoulder to shoulder with important people they might never have met.

For ex-soldiers who joined the ranks, and for many who had been too young to serve in the Confederate Army, here was an opportunity to enjoy the thrills of war without its terrible risks. Since cowardly Klansmen—in overwhelming numbers—attacked from ambush or at night and quickly rode off, they did not face the terrible dangers of real soldiers.

The Ku Klux Klan was never a centralized organization, but rather a loose set of marauding bands united behind a general purpose. Dens did not apply for charters, receive instructions from a national office or have much contact with one another. No one is sure what Nathan Bedford Forrest did for the various Dens, and they hardly needed guidance from above.

Whether in Mississippi, Texas or Arkansas, Klansmen operated in the same way. They armed and deployed in small groups of half a dozen or larger groups of several dozen men. They made sure they outnum-bered their victims and then used death threats, random violence and finally systematic torture and murders to instill fear and shock in their victims.

Toward Black people, including women and children, they acted in

The first Black Senator, and Congressmen in the 41st and 42nd Congress of the United States. Senator Hiram R. Revels of Mississippi; and Representatives Benjamin S. Turner of Alabama; Robert C. De Large of South Carolina; Josiah T. Walls of Florida; Jefferson F. Long of Georgia; Joseph H. Rainy of South Carolina; Robert B. Elliott of South Carolina.

barbaric ways, and this was purposeful. First, it brought terror home to every family, and acted as a terrible pressure on the Black male voter. Second, treating Black families in unspeakably cruel ways was a statement that they were inferior and neither their pain nor death mattered.

From its first foray into their lives, Klan terrorism became a family matter for Blacks. Black families discussed what each member would do when the hooded riders came around. Children served as look-outs, women protected guns and ammunition, and the elderly tried to confuse the mounted terrorists with false directions and misinformation. The adult men and sometimes the older children became soldiers in defense of their families.

Klan raiders immediately faced opposition. No one knows the name of that Black woman in Tennessee who clashed with the two Klansmen who entered her home. All that is known for sure is that she chased them out with a broom, and some say the men kept running all the way to the state line.

In the years that followed, Klansmen were driven off by determined

Black women and men, some armed with rifles, knives and swords, but others only swinging brooms and pitchforks. Rather than recall these humiliations, Klansmen laughingly told tales of how Black people, frightened at their ghost-like appearance, had fled into the woods. Those who fled the marauders were not frightened by appearances, but by the bulging guns beneath their sheets, and by a knowledge of their murderous record.

The Invisible Empire's leaders realized their task required an overwhelming force. What gray-coated armies failed to win on the battlefields of the Civil War, Klan raiders tried to achieve through terrorist violence. Over the next decade, untold thousands of innocent people died or were injured in wars waged by the Invisible Empire. Most were Black.

The leading targets of The Invisible Empire were the most successful Black figures on the political landscape. Klansmen selected these imposing southern people because their mere presence refuted White supremacy claims. From 1870 to 1898, 22 Black men, including two Senators from Mississippi, were elected to the U.S. Congress. Hundreds of others served effectively as deputy sheriffs, tax collectors, school principals, city councilmen, state legislators, Secretarys of State, Lieutenant-Governors and Justices of state Supreme Courts.

Klan activities were aimed at destroying their effectiveness, ruining their careers, wrecking their property, driving them from their homes, or silencing them forever. What could not be accomplished through violence, could be achieved through false stories planted in newspapers, whisper campaigns, denial of credit and banks loans, wives and relatives denied work, and threats to and assaults on children walking to or from school.

In the North, papers offered their readers little news about the daily mayhem sweeping the South, and confused the issue of who were the promoters, and who were the sufferers. In the South, hardly anyone White dared intervene to stop the slaughter. Local authorities claimed they were helpless in the face of enormous atrocities and did nothing. An undermanned US Army and a politically divided US Congress exchanged charges of blame for the failure to halt the mayhem. Meanwhile the violence continued.

In 1871, Congress finally admitted it was facing "a rebellion against the government of the United States," began a full investigation and passed laws to halt the Klan. Even then the terror did not stop.

How terrorist riders of The Invisible Empire were able to wield such power, defy US authority and dominate so much of the South is a fascinating story. Why the Federal government with unlimited resources and manpower was unable to stop these night-riders is an American tragedy no less fascinating.

4

THE INVISIBLE EMPIRE
RIDES INTO POLITICS

THE U.S. PRESIDENTIAL ELECTION OF 1868 gave The Invisible Empire its first opportunity to demonstrate the political power of massive terrorism. The Republican Party nominated General U.S. Grant, the popular war hero. The Democrats nominated Governor Horatio Seymore of New York.

The Klan rode into ten southern states as the violent cutting edge of the Seymore campaign. From Virignia to Texas, half a million men saddled up under a variety of names, and sometimes no name at all. In Louisiana, they were the Knights of the White Camellia, in Texas, Knights of the Rising Sun, in Mississippi, The White Line, and elsewhere the Pale Faces, White Brotherhood, Seymore Knights or The Invisible Empire. Some communities had more than one masked band of night-riders.

Everywhere the aim, tactics and message were the same. By any means necessary, these masked men meant to capture the White House for Seymore and the Democrats. Republicans and Black voters had better beware!

Klan methods first stressed various kinds of intimidation. Klan threats were printed in local papers, posted on trees in the countryside, or bulletin boards in towns. They warned White and Black Republicans to leave town, or to change sides or stay at home on election day. To emphasize their point, masked gunmen paraded past Republican meetings and the homes of prominent Black and White leaders. When this failed to stampede foes, Klan riders set fires to barns, homes and meeting halls.

Since there was no secret ballot at the time, it was not difficult to intimidate voters. Before the election, each party distributed ballots, one color for Democrats, another for Republicans, that voters carried to the polling box. But what Republicans handed out, Klansmen forcefully collected.

Black voters, as the most vulnerable, became special Klan targets. Masked riders rode out to Black homes, seized all weapons, and warned men not to vote. Rarely during this first visit were men, women and children injured or killed. They were usually given a clear warning, and sometimes beaten. Bloody or not, this time, the hooded marauders announced the next visit would be unbearable for any family boasting a Republican voter.

A Klan visit immediately turned one man's voting right into a family matter and a community project. First husband and wife had to discuss how to meet the crisis. Women, children, fathers, brothers, grand-parents, aunts and uncles talked of the consequences. Neighbors helped shape fateful decisions.

In the weeks before election day, Klan terror and violence peaked. Three or four times a night masked riders galloped off to besiege the homes of Black Republicans. Some voters had learned enough about The Invisible Empire to be hiding in wooded areas. Those found at home were called out and sometimes adult men or their wives and children were abused or slain. When people refused to come out, Klansmen set homes ablaze. By election day, many Black families had been sleeping in the woods near their homes for weeks or months.

The Klan's stormy violence was only the raucous side of the Democratic campaign strategy. The other, equally important part, was contributed by respectable judges , sheriffs and grand jurors. They had joined or were sympathetic to Klan goals. They looked the other way or refused to raise a cautious hand against the escalating terror.

Some lawmen, out of sympathy or fearing for their lives, joined the hooded order. Sheriffs would not organize posses to chase after lawless bands; they would not arrest The Invisible Empire's known law-breakers. If a Klan member was arrested, his friends testified that he was somewhere else on the day or night in question, and he was speedily released. Even Klansmen caught red-handed were released by the justice system and never came to trial. Judges refused to take sworn testimony by Black victims, and dismissed the words of White Republicans.

Democratic Party papers published the names of Republican voters, providing a convenient enemies list for stores, banks and schools.

Black politician campaigning.

Republican wives found they could not easily shop, gain credit at stores or assume their school children were safe. To travel lonely roads or enter unfriendly towns, they rightly feared, might invite a Klan ambush.

On election day, Klan violence and legal authorities united to form a powerful opposition fist. Polls were suddenly and secretly moved to locations known only to Democrats. Armed Klansmen blocked roads leading to polling booths, and judges failed to issue orders clearing the roads. Masked raiders fired into crowds of Black citizens. Sheriffs arrived too late to make arrests, or simply refused to act against criminals.

Election day became a terrifying, unpredictable nightmare for Republican voters. Planters and overseers refused to grant time off to laborers. Republican voters were told they might lose jobs or homes. Families were warned fathers, brothers and uncles might never return.

On the way to the polls, voters were stopped by armed men, or fired on by sharpshooters. Once on line they faced mounted Klansmen waving rifles and shouting warnings. Blacks who carried weapons were disarmed by the local sheriffs or the Klan, or could be arrested for provoking disorder.

After voting ended, Republican ballots might be seized by hooded men. Voting and getting home alive for Republicans in heavily Klan districts became an act of courage, and something of a miracle. Unfortunately, the bravest individual had to worry about the perils he was creating that day for an unprotected family. When he finally returned home, would he find his loved ones safe?

Even when the ballots were cast and the polls closed, the election was not over. Republican poll-watchers were chased away from the polls when the counting began. Once the polls were closed, Democratic local officials miscounted or destroyed Republican ballots. By the time Republicans returned with court orders, ballots were missing and the tabulating was finished. Not to be outdone, Republicans retaliated with similar election frauds and manipulations.

To shield their fraud and violence, Klansmen relied on local authorities. Since most people knew who they were anyway, this was a far more crucial protection than the hoods hiding their identities. Some lawmen listened to citizens who reported crimes, and routinely passed all information on to the local Klan. Supported by the law, encouraged by prominent citizens, The Invisible Empire governed vast southern regions.

The only other force that could have halted The Invisible Empire was the U.S. Army. The 25,000 troops assigned to the South also had to guard a restless Rio Grande border with Mexico. They had too many criminals to watch, too many miles to cover, too many conflicting orders to follow.

Northern White officers and men were hardly enthusiastic about fighting White men who wanted to stop "black domination." The U.S. Army became an unreliable, confused, overworked guardian of racial equality. For these and other reasons, it proved unable to halt the Ku Klux Klan.

Even had the U.S. armed forces stood ready to enforce the law of the land, they would have faced enormous legal and other difficulties. The criminals they would have arrested came from the best White southern families. The Invisible Empire united common criminals and sons of the landed aristocracy, merchants and vagrants, laborers and the children of judges. A reporter in the South for the Cincinnati *Gazette* wrote:

34

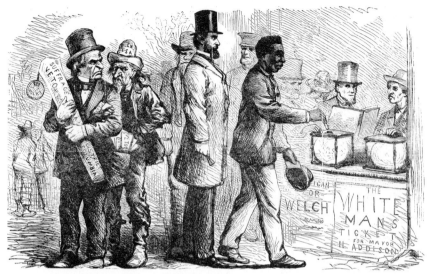

Thomas Nast cartoon of 1867 depicting Whites, including President Andrew Johnson, watching a new Black voter.

Were all the Ku Klux arrested and brought to trial, among them would be found sheriffs, magistrates, jurors and legislators, and it may be clerks and judges.

The marauders had the support of most local newspapers. These kept up a steady drumbeat against "Black Republicanism." When the *Iliad* in Louisiana dared tell how the Klan victimized White and Black Republicans—"men dogged and hunted down to death"—a mob destroyed its office and press.

Clarence Collier, a Klan assassin at 21, became a hero when he shotgunned a Kansas lawman in the back and then pumped shells into his writhing body. Because his victim was a Republican, the *Memphis* Leader wrote:

Gallant Clarence Collier! The blessings of an oppressed people go with you and whenever the clouds lift you shall be known and honored throughout the land. . . .

35

In 1868, one southern community after another found that Klan terror destroyed law and order. In Alabama, a Republican complained of murders "daily and nightly—and nobody is found out, arrested or punished. The civil authority is seemingly powerless—the military does not act—and the whole thing goes on, and is getting worse."

In Louisiana, justice spun out of control and the Governor pleaded with Blacks who wanted to save their lives. . .not to vote. Klansmen in Louisiana rounded up Blacks at gunpoint and forced them to vote the Democratic ticket. One district after another in Louisiana reported no Republican votes. In a district where one Black man voted, he was found slain a month later.

In Jefferson, Texas, Major James Curtis of the US Army and 26 soldiers tried hard to protect Black and White Republicans. Gunfights erupted between criminal bands and Republicans. Casualties mounted. When the sheriff arrested Republicans, a Klan mob of 70 descended on the prison, drove off U.S. soldiers on guard, and massacred some of the prisoners.

The best Major Curtis could do was escort the survivors out of town the next day. One paper called the slaughter an "unavoidable necessity" for "the peace and safety of society."

Only in Arkansas, where Klansmen were fewer, did they meet their match. Klansmen escalated their violence. They murdered a White Congressman from Little Rock, and another White politician had to sleep in the woods for a month to avoid assassination. Governor Powell Clayton, shocked at 200 Klan slayings, declared war. He armed Black and White militiamen, sent spies into The Invisible Empire and prepared for bloodshed.

He also prepared a special assault on the criminals. When a Colonel Pickett marched into his office claiming "there are no Ku Klux in Woodruff county," the Governor reached into his desk and produced a list of prominent Klansmen—with the Colonel's name first. A shaken Pickett agreed to disband his Den.

Taking the offensive, Clayton ordered his militia into battle, and the secret order fell back. Klan murders dropped from 200 to five. Military trials jailed Klan officials and the violence screeched to a halt in Arkansas. Other states were not so lucky.

Thomas Nast cartoon of 1868 revealing the cost of bigotry for Black southern families (Harper's Weekly)

The Presidential election of 1868 saw U.S. Grant elected to the White House despite the Klan. However, night-riders of The Invisible Empire successfully drove Georgia and Louisiana into the Democratic camp, and sharply reduced Republican majorities in eight other states. Many local officials friendly to or fearful of the masked raiders were elected.

Klan terror vividly demonstrated the political power of fear. After all, boasted a Klan that had spread death across a broad landscape, this was only a first try—the Klan was still young.

No one will ever know how many died or were wounded for daring to vote or run for office in 1868. They numbered in the thousands. US General Edward Hatch wrote "Although my report is dark with these atrocities, I can safely say that hundreds are not yet reported and a great many never will be." In addition, many innocent southern Black women and children suffered savage cruelty or painful death because their husbands and fathers marched to the polls carrying Republican ballots.

As a triumphant U.S. Grant prepared to enter the White House, General Forrest issued a confusing Klan directive. Claiming "bad men" had infiltrated The Invisible Empire, he announced that Klan activities, masks and disguises would be abandoned. Was this just a ploy to mislead those fed up with Klan atrocities? The Dens appeared to vanish in Texas, Arkansas and Louisiana, but elsewhere masked riders saddled up as before.

In the 1868 Presidential election, The Invisible Empire left its first violent imprint on the national heritage. With crucial help from prominent local citizens and lawmen, the night-riders proved capable of wrecking or crippling large parts of the democratic process. In many localities, intimidation and murder surely cut down the resolve and the votes of unarmed people.

The Klan knew that men who went to sleep with fright and awoke to terror would think twice about voting. In Jones County, North Carolina, during the election violence, a group of citizens wrote their Governor "We cannot tell at night who will be living in the morning."

5

ASSAULT ON SOUTHERN
LIFE AND JUSTICE

THOSE WHO DONNED HOODS AND SHEETS to wage war for White supremacy were interested in more than winning elections. They carried forth a program to force ex-slaves "into their place"—under White domination. They saw any instance of Black advancement as a threat, and any successful Black man or woman as a knife poised at the throat of White society. Since Black people determined to see their freedom meant just that, Klansmen and Blacks were on a collision course.

William Coleman found that out late one night when eight masked men crashed into his home. Ex-slave Coleman became a prosperous farmer, then joined the Republican Party because it promised freedom and opportunity. He was proud of his success, proud of his state of Mississippi and proud of his party.

But Coleman had become a Klan target without knowing it. The armed men who pushed into his home were upset about more than his prosperity. As they beat and shot at him, one yelled he was "going about like you thought yourself a white man!" Another shouted "God damn you, when you meet a white man in the road lift your hat!"

Coleman told a Congressional Committee that he had other friends who had been attacked by armed men because "they had land" or "they had got too big" in Klan eyes. The Invisible Empire became interested in suppressing every instance of Black economic equality or pride. Klansmen beat Black women for dressing in brightly-colored clothes, and men for being impolite, talking back to Whites or failing to say "Yes, Sir."

Southern planters enlisted the aid of the Klan to keep control of their workers, keep their wages low and break strikes. "The nigger is going to be made a serf, sure as you live," promised a rich Alabama planter. Economic control of Black labor was key to White supremacy figures.

Hooded Klansmen threatened outspoken Black sharecropper lead-

39

ers, and rode back to murder those who would not knuckle under. When it came time to pay sharecroppers, the planters hired Klansmen to drive them away. "Driving the freedom from their crops and seizing it themselves when it is grown, is a complaint against the planters that comes to us from every quarter," a US Army officer reported from Texas.

Klansmen in North Carolina, furious that an elderly White man had given his former slaves some land, surrounded him one cold night on

A Black man is thrown out of a restaurant after slavery had ended.

a country road. They cut off his clothes with a knife, whipped him and left the naked man to walk five miles to his home. In Florida, Klan raiders set fire to crops owned by Blacks and fired at some Whites who sold them the farming land.

A key Klan goal aimed to keep Blacks from owning land. Only by keeping a White monopoly of the land, they reasoned, would Blacks be kept in their place. "Keep them poor and dependent," explained one White, "was the only possible way to get along with colored people." Owning land became, for Blacks, a courageous act of defiance, and it often made them Klan targets.

Blacks who entered new trades and professions also attracted the angry attention of White supremacists. In Alabama, Klansmen whipped

Black railroad firemen, chased Black railroad workers off their jobs and shot at Black mail agents. When the Red River Iron Company in Kentucky hired Black men, KKK terror closed it down.

A former slave in Texas summarized his peoples' economic state after slavery: "We soon found out that freedom could make folks proud, but it couldn't make them rich."

Denied the right to learn to read and write during slavery, education became a leading goal of the ex-slaves. Before the guns of the Civil War ended, Black people were teaching one another and their children the magic of reading, writing and arithmetic. "I consider education the next best thing to liberty," said one ex-slave. In Georgia, another said "Thank God I have a book now. The lord has sent us books and teachers. We must not hesitate a moment, but go on and learn all we can."

Congress enacted a Freedmen's Bureau Law that established more than 4,000 schools, hired more than 10,000 teachers and raised Black literacy from 5% to 25% in five years. Religious denominations also sent hundreds of teachers and thousands of books into the South. "They are *crazy* to learn," wrote one Bureau official. "They will starve themselves, and go without clothes in order to send their children to school," wrote another.

Before northern religious societies or the Freedmen's Bureau arrived to build schools, Black parents were raising money for them and constructing them with their own hands. Schools were a success because Black parents made sacrifices to support them. "We work all day but we'll come to you in the evening for learning," Black Georgia plantation laborers told a White teacher. In North Carolina, a Bureau official reported this unusual scene: "A child six years old, her mother, grandmother and great grandmother, the latter over 75 years of age . . . commenced their alphabet together and each one can read the Bible fluently."

White supremacists saw educated Black adults and children as a clear threat to their goals, and they rode out to destroy schools and drive off teachers. A White Waco, Texas, paper warned "we do not approve . . . making them smart and like White folks."

Black parents hoped their children's education would lead them up the economic ladder of success. Jealous Whites feared exactly that would happen and poor Whites would be pushed further down the scale of failure. The long Klan war against the schools took many casualties. "The record of the teachers of the first colored schools in Louisiana will be one of honor and blood," wrote the New Orleans *Tribune*.

Teachers sometimes had to flee for their lives or face whipping, branding or death for instructing Black children. In one Mississippi county, 11 schools were burned down, and not one left in operation. In another county, 26 schools were closed by Klan violence and threats. In Walton, Georgia, night-riders burned a teacher's books and told his students to get rid of their books "or else."

Black people tried mightily to protect their schools and defend their teachers. White teachers, refused homes in the White community, were given lodging and protection in the Black community.

Students stood by their teachers when Klan assaults threatened and resistance took many forms. In Marianna, Florida, a White teacher was called out of his classroom one night by a masked mob and threatened with guns. His students rushed out and chased the mob away. When the mob returned to burn down the school, some 40 armed Black students and friends arrived, and the mob muttered and dispersed. In Mississippi, Black Sunday school teacher Samuel Allen fought off an armed mob with a saber, and then fled to the woods.

Whites who fostered Black education faced increasing Klan attack. Robert Flournoy of Mississippi originally planned to build integrated schools, but he soon determined that his state would never permit that. Instead he used his own money to start 52 White and 12 Black schools. Confronted one night by a Klan assassination squad of 30, Flournoy and eight of his friends were fired on but escaped.

The Invisible Empire was determined to close down Flournoy's schools one way or another. Mounted horsemen rode off and set his schools ablaze. Pleased local Whites elected the Grand Cyclops the new sheriff, and Klansmen kept Flournoy's schools a target in Mississippi.

As Klan violence continued year after year, the real victim became

Black children running off to the new southern public schools. (Harper's Weekly)

the delicate process of legal justice. Klansmen "have the law and the courts all on their side. The juries were made up of Ku-Klux, and it was impossible for any of the loyal people to get justice before the courts," reported Colonel George Kirk of North Carolina's Militia. In Alabama, U.S. General Crawford said "The whole civil system is poisoned to the core. Fear seems to have possessed executive men, and intimidation controls the avenues of justice."

For southern Blacks, justice under either Republicans or Democrats was a sorry joke. For committing the same crimes as Whites, they were consistently handed longer sentences, and were sent to jail for crimes that Whites were punished with small fines. Blacks were executed for crimes that merely put Whites in jail and convicted for crimes that did not apply to Whites: "being uppity," "insulting Whites" and "being disrespectful."

Sheriffs rarely arrested Whites for even serious crimes against Blacks. Many Black men and women gave up reporting crimes, even serious assaults and murders, since lawmen did nothing. The Invisible Empire succeeded in making entire sections of the South hotbeds of crime with minimal legal protection for anyone but the very rich.

In this atmosphere, outlaw bands flourished. In Texas, an official reported the presence of White gangs who "kill negroes for the pure love of killing." In Georgia, marauders were reported "murdering whole families." In many places, authorities permitted so much bloodshed that community order veered out of control. Lawmen feared to arrest criminals.

In time, the crime wave became so pervasive that even Klansmen claimed "bad men" had joined their order and given it a bad name. David Schenck, a Georgia Klan leader, quit in disgust saying the organization had "degenerated into a band of robbers, rioters and lynch lawmen." When he served as commander, he had proclaimed his belief in "the extinction of the negro race." But now, according to Schenck, it was chaos because its criminals threatened White people.

By the early 1870s, Dens of The Invisible Empire, as one member said, "began to take law in our own hands, to whip anyone we thought had done anything mean." Alabama Klansmen attacked mountain Whites they considered "deviant Methodists." Kentucky Dens took

After the Civil War the Freedmen's Bureau was established by the Federal government to keep the peace, but it lasted only five years. (Harper's Weekly)

sides in family feuds. In Tennessee, Klansmen lynched a Jewish storekeeper who tried to defend his Black employee when the Klan came around. One Kentucky Den tried to burn down a community of Shakers, a religious minority.

The Invisible Empire, immersed in violence, easily slipped into random atrocities and murders. Their crimes shocked entire communities and at times crushed not the desire but the ability to fight back. Black and White families, with what weapons they had, battled the KKK in each locality and state. They won temporary victories and for varying amounts of time, slowed down the Klan's murderous drive. But since Klansmen could arrive unexpectedly at night, commit their crimes and ride off with no lawmen in pursuit, they were almost impossible to stop.

The impact of The Invisible Empire cannot be measured simply in body counts or people driven away from their homes. Any assessment of their damage over vast regions of the southland must also count careers stunted, hopes blighted, and normal development crippled. Worst, this devastation lasted for decades.

Facing Klan armies that sought their overthrow, Governors in all southern states except Virginia and Georgia recruited military companies. Though they included Whites, most were so largely filled with Black volunteers that they were known as Black militias. Commissioned officers were White. For young Blacks who crowded the ranks, their eager service meant guarding the state and protecting their families and freedom. These state forces, despite their lack of training, strategic failures and occasional poor judgment, were often crucial in protecting the democratic election process.

This KKK notice was published in an Atlanta paper in 1868, warning those northerners who came to the south to help Blacks that they faced lynching if they did not leave.

[From the Independent Monitor, Tuscaloosa, Alabama, September 1, 1868.]
A PROSPECTIVE SCENE IN THE CITY OF OAKS, 4TH OF MARCH, 1869.

"Hang, curs, hang! * * * * * *   *Their* complexion is perfect gallows. Stand fast, good fate, to *their* hanging!   If they be not born to be hanged, our case is miserable."
The above cut represents the fate in store for those great pests of Southern society—the carpet-bagger and scalawag—if found in Dixie's land after the break of day on the 4th of March next.

A Facsimile put in Evidence before the Congressional Committee.

These military units aroused White fears, stirred intense local opposition and soon generated political controversy. Klan figures harped on this Black military presence as proof that White lives and property were no longer safe.

Klansmen recorded the names of Black militia leaders in "Dead Books," or paraded their coffins-to-be—marked "Dead, damned and delivered"—through towns. Klan assassination squads singled out and lynched those who had answered their state's call.

But as long as the militia companies lasted, they served notice to Klansmen that they could no longer ride out and destroy communities without risking their lives. Finally, the Governors who called them into existence, persuaded that this Black army might ignite racial war, disbanded them.

For a century, the saga of the Black militia companies reached the public through the words of their Klan enemies. According to Klan interpretations, not law and order, not protection of the state, but rule, rape and robbery were the goals. This distortion permeated school and popular histories for the next century.

This version served as the tense setting to the silent movie classic, *The Birth of a Nation*. It portrayed strutting, leering Black soldiers riding off to rape "the flower of southern womanhood" and plunder society. In this way, the film justified the Klan's birth. In actuality, Klan violence came first, and left Governors no choice but to form defensive Black companies.

6

A SOUTHERN DREAM
TURNS NIGHTMARE

BY THE CONGRESSIONAL ELECTIONS OF 1870, the Republicans had become worried about the Klan menace in the South. They were not concerned with the mounting body count of dead Republican supporters. Most were Black. Their fear was that Klan power, if unchecked, might deny President Grant his re-election to the White House in two years.

Since The Invisible Empire's violence soared and fell and rose again, Republicans also faced criticism for their handling of the South. Voters were alarmed that trouble danced under the noses of the US Army, and defied Federal authority. Some Northerners wanted the Klan firmly crushed. Others who believed a return of "White supremacy" would bring peace and save tax money, wanted Federal troops withdrawn.

Unless something was done, Republican reconstruction policies could insure a massive defection of voters to the Democrats. Since their grip on the Federal government was threatened unless the Klan violence was halted, Republicans devised a new plan. Its aim was to prevent a Democratic "solid South"—from which the party could ride back into control of the national government.

Republicans viewed the staggering loss of lives as an embarrassment that reflected on policy weaknesses. Any remorse for voters slain or intimidated stemmed not from human emotions, but because they could not vote Republican. Since Klan intimidation and murders could spell doom for Republican rule in the South, something had to be done before the next Presidential election.

Beginning in the election year of 1870, the US Congress passed four Anti-Klan laws. Congressmen and the President hoped that the mere passage of these laws would frighten the Klansmen and enforcement would be unnecessary. They were wrong. The tornado of violence continued. Congess then ordered a thorough investigation of Southern conditions.

President Grant also ordered his own investigation to be conducted by the US Army. He dispatched Major Lewis Merrill and troops of the Seventh US Cavalry into York County, South Carolina, where terror gripped the population. Rumors of bloodshed rolled out of York and the President wanted to know if the Klan was responsible for the violence.

There was real confusion in the public mind. Newspapers in the North and South had claimed that either a KKK did not exist or stories about its horrendous activities were exaggerated. Superstitious Black people, some papers insisted, had spread scandalous lies about a secret organization designed to protect White people from "blacks running amok."

Major Merrill arrived with a typical Northern attitude about The Invisible Empire—he knew little, suspected the violence was blown out of proportion, and thought the KKK a hoax. In three months, as his own investigation piled up a mountain of evidence, he changed his mind.

So bold had The Invisible Empire become that ten days after Merrill arrived, it launched a series of raids. In nine months, 11 more people died and 600 were injured. Four Black schools and churches were burned to the ground, and one was torn down and had to be rebuilt four times. Nightly entire Black communities in York slept in the woods, and others felt safe by bedding down near Merrill's Yorkville Army headquarters.

Merrill began his investigation by interviewing leading citizens who denied Klan crimes or who claimed there was no such organization. But soon he was listening to harrowing tales by White and Black Klan victims. Since he could hardly believe the atrocities they told him, he sent his own spies into the hooded order. Only then did he realize the worst was true—the richest and "best citizens" of York organized the terror.

Klansmen, he concluded, were cowards hiding behind their disguises and using overwhelming numbers and firepower to destroy democratic government. More evil than the mounted raiders were York's leading citizens who manipulated The Invisible Empire. Merrill wrote:

I am now of the opinion that I never conceived of such a state of social disorganization being possible in a civilized community as exists in this country now.

Local officials refused to indict or arrest criminals. Merrill's Federal orders forbade him to act against state offenses such as murder, arson and mutilation. His frustration made him furious: "It requires great patience and self control to keep one's hands off these infamous cowards, when absolute knowledge exists of who they are, and what they do, and what they propose to do."

Merrill bided his time, kept his secret agents busy, and left his office door open to anyone with a tale to tell. People found he could be trusted and many came by to sit and talk.

Masked raiders, on a regular schedule that targeted a different neighborhood each night, rode out to intimidate Republican (which by then, in York, meant Black) voters. Merrill knew conditions were becoming chaotic when he heard Blacks were arming for war. He also learned from Klan insiders that "the lowest-down, meanest characters that we have among us" were now directing activities.

Yet Merrill could not act until President Grant and Congress untied his hands. With all his arms and men, he remained without authorization to intervene in state matters.

Neither Congress nor the President wanted to admit that their policies had failed in the South. Neither wanted to inform the American public that greater legal and military intervention was necessary. Years after the war ended, it was not advisable to request tax money so soldiers could guard Blacks from White people. Besides, this admission of failure could lose Northern districts to the Democrats. These political considerations overshadowed any pain and sorrow in the South.

President Grant received Major Merrill's investigative reports and Senator John Scott made sure the President read them. Scott then began his own Senate Committee inquiry into The Invisible Empire. Klansmen, Merrill discovered from his spies, read his secret reports to the War Department and the White House before they arrived in Washington.

If the Grant Administration proved unwilling to act on the crimes

Congressman Robert B. Elliott of South Carolina addressing Congress on civil rights. (Library of Congress)

Major Merrill had exposed, the 1870 elections changed its mind. Increased Klan terrorism drove Georgia and Alabama into the Democratic column and slashed Republican majorities by the thousands in the southern states. Unless it acted decisively, the party would have no future in the South.

With Merrill's reports and reams of congressional testimony in his hands, Senator Scott repeatedly pressed the President for action. It was a time of anguish for Grant and the Republicans.

Finally the President made his choice, and suddenly Major Merrill had 400 soldiers at his command and orders to begin prosecutions under the Ku Klux Klan acts. Grant sent Attorney General Amos Aker-

Black communities had to sleep in the woods for weeks and months to escape Klan assaults. (Harper's Weekly)

man to help Merrill sift through evidence and plan Federal criminal indictments.

Major Merrill had done his homework well, and had kept open his lines of communication to the York community. He was on friendly, talking terms with leading Klansmen, their Black victims and the "best citizens" of the town. He dispatched the Seventh Cavalry, not the local sheriff, to serve warrants. The sheriff, Merrill had found out, had been a Klansman all along.

Warrants in their saddle bags, Merrill's Cavalrymen fanned out over the countryside. To his surprise, Merrill found members of The Invisible Empire crowding into his office offering to confess and implicate others in exchange for leniency. The Klan called those who turned in friends "pukers," but "pukers" came forward every week. Said Merrill:

> Day after day, for weeks, men came in such numbers that time
> to hear them confess and means to dispose of or take care of
> them both failed, and I was powerless to do anything more than
> secure the persons of those most deeply criminal, and send the

rest to their homes on their personal parole. . . .In some instances whole Klans, headed by their chief, came in and surrendered together.

The defendants enjoyed the best legal talent the South had to offer. Future Senators, Supreme Court Justices and Cabinet ministers, serving as attorneys for the accused, argued forcefully that The Invisible Empire was organized to combat corruption and crime, and save the South from "black political and social domination."

The Federal attorneys presented overwhelming evidence of a massive political conspiracy to undermine the democratic process by terrorizing entire communities. Major Merrill's witnesses proved beyond any doubt that the Klan had systematically utilized weapons of torture and death. The American public read of Klan atrocities they could hardly believe. At one point, a Klan lawyer, shocked at the testimony on atrocities, leaped to his feet and denounced the secret order.

Because the courts became so clogged with Klan trials, many of the guilty went free. In order to bring the worst offenders to court, others never reached the bar of justice. In addition, thousands of criminals received suspended sentences or short prison terms. Some wealthy men escaped justice by fleeing the state or to Canada, and only returned when prosecutions ended.

Merrill became convinced that without more Federal judges, the guilty would never face punishment. Congress refused to pass the law he requested and justice slowed down. Attorney General Akerman resigned, some believed, because the Grant Administration would not prosecute enough criminals. Merrill saw many Klansmen slip through his carefully woven legal net.

Perhaps he had failed to understand that the aim of the President and Congress was political. They wanted to smash The Invisible Empire, not punish Klansmen. With the Klan terror halted, Republicans could carry southern states and elect their candidates. Sensational trials that cast hundreds of White citizens in jail were not popular.

Convicted felons often were placed on probation rather than in prison and sent back to their families. Almost as soon as the jail door clanged shut on the first convicted Klan members, a clemency campaign began. Prominent citizens urged a generous "mercy" as the best path to racial harmony. Merrill vigorously battled early pardons for convicted criminals.

Merrill's fear was that leniency would encourage the very men capable of cranking up a new Invisible Empire. The first who returned home from jail were the richest and most influential Klansmen, those who had directed the fiery avalanche.

The Major's office continued to buzz with people giving their reactions to the events shaking their community. Some respectable citizens voiced outrage that Klansmen were in court instead of home with their families. But others cautiously admitted that the trials were necessary to restore a sense of public decency and a conscience deadened by Klan rule.

Based on the models Merrill and Akerman established in York County, Klan prosecutions spread to other southern states. Under siege by Federal prosecutors, The Invisible Empire disbanded and its leaders faced victims, juries and judges.

Striding erect and fearless to the witness stand, Black and White women and men who had been victimized, finally had their day in court. The guilty could no longer hide behind their white masks and disguises, or their influential friends. Witnesses exposed brutal crimes and sometimes saw their tormentors whisked to jail. Punishment was mild and haphazard. For committing hundreds of murders, brandings and whippings in North Carolina, only 37 went to jail—most for a year or less.

For the Grant Administration, the political approach to the Klan trials was rewarding. In 1872, the President was returned to power in a quiet, orderly election. By 1875, all Klan prisoners, except the most recently convicted, were home.

Northern White opinion, Republican leaders, Congressmen, and the President had never been enthusiastic about the racial experiment in the South. Northern politicians viewed their new southern Black allies as expendable.

Congress never considered confiscation and division of the South's huge plantations. This radical step would have cut down the Klan's support; it would have struck a blow at those who launched the rebellion and financed the Klan; it would have provided southern Black

Black men, convicted of minor crimes, became the unpaid labor reserve. These men were forced to build roads in North Carolina in 1910. (Library of Congress)

and White voters with the economic independence they desperately needed. Instead, the South's poor became sharecroppers, endlessly chained to land and jobs owned by their exploiters.

The Black-White governments installed by Congress toppled one by one. By 1874, only South Carolina, Florida, Mississippi and Louisiana remained. They tensely waited for the merciless day when their Federal troops would be withdrawn. They did not wait long.

In 1875, Mississippi experienced massive electoral violence that left a trail of corpses. "We are in the hands of murderers," wrote 300 Black Vicksburg voters. Mississippi "is governed today by officials chosen through fraud and violence. . .savages," said President Grant. But Presidents would no longer act to halt White atrocities. The next year in South Carolina a bloody "Red Shirt" campaign drove out its Black-White rulers.

In 1876, Klan-like electoral violence and fraud cut a path so wide through the South, it was unclear who had won the White House. A compromise offered by a Congressional election commission granted the White House to Republican Hayes. He agreed to withdraw all Federal troops and restore "Home Rule."

By the time Hayes left the White House, a totalitarian system governed each state of the old Confederacy. The Ku Klux Klan had been defeated, but its goals had been achieved and its banner flew over 11 states. From Virginia to Texas, the old aristocracy that once owned the most land and slaves, again controlled state and local governments and picked US Senators.

A new arrangement made business partners of northern industrialists and bankers who directed the Republican Party, and White aristocrats who ran the South. The Republican's earlier allies were Black and penniless; the new partners were people of their own class and culture.

The Klan toll on lives taken and ruined was staggering. It is not possible to tabulate the number of women, men and children killed or wounded by this multi-state atrocity. The casualties probably reached into the thousands.

In a January 10, 1875 letter from New Orleans, General Philip Sheridan wrote of the death toll in Louisiana:

> Since the year 1866, nearly 3500 persons, a great majority of which were colored men, have been killed and wounded in this state. In 1868 the official record shows that 1884 were killed and wounded. From 1868 to the present time no official investigation had been made and the civil authorities, in all by a few cases, have been unable to arrest, convict or punish the perpetrators; consequently there are no correct records to be consulted for information.
>
> There is ample evidence, however, to show that more than 1200 persons have been killed and wounded during this time, on account of their political sentiments. Frightful massacres have occurred. . . . Human life in this state is held so cheaply that . . . murderers are regarded rather as heroes than as criminals in the localities in which they reside.

No assessment can ever be made of those mothers, fathers, daughters, sons, cousins, uncles, aunts, and grandparents driven to grief or mad-ness by what they saw or suffered. To escape the carnage, thousands were forced to pick up their belongings and leave beloved homelands.

Still, 90% of the Black population remained in the South living there under a rigid tyranny. With White supremacy in power there was little need for an Invisible Empire. Those who rode horseback in white sheets and hoods now sat as judges, jurors and Senators or as sheriffs and deputies. The Invisible Empire faded away, not because it had been defeated, but because it had won.

Congressman George Henry White, an ex-slave, introduced the first anti-lynching bill to Congress on January 20, 1900.

White lynch mobs, led by elected officials and rarely hiding behind masks, terrorized Black communities. The South's Senators, Governors and ministers justified violence in the name of defending "white womanhood." A White North no longer wanted to hear about "the nigger question in the South."

The Black South was terrified but never pacified. Black church figures voiced demands for justice. Huge migrations tried to move Black communities to Kansas, Oklahoma or to Africa—anywhere to escape oppression. In North Carolina, the Lowrie guerrilla band united three races against Klan-like violence. In Georgia's Liberty county, a thousand armed Blacks liberated Henry Delagal from arrest, hid him in the swamps and defied regiments of Georgia militiamen. Even the number of grisly southern lynchings—reaching three or four a week in 1892—demonstrated an undying, gritty Black resistance.

In some states, Blacks continued to elect men to office—at the time of the "Delegal riots" Liberty county, Georgia had two Blacks in the state assembly. From 1877 until 1900, when ex-slave George H. White of North Carolina was forced to leave because it became legally impossible for him to seek reelection, at least one Black man served a term in the U.S. Congress. In his farewell speech, White predicted his people would rise from the ashes and return to Congress.

A New Klan
for a New Time:
1915 to 1929

7

AN AGE OF
SUSPICION AND FEAR

THE OLD KLAN LAY BURIED FOR HALF a century but many times its spirit rose from a shallow grave to roam free. It abandoned its regional approach and discovered many evildoers besides "uppity" Blacks. The era between the 1870s and 1916 gave it new targets and a great deal of fuel.

At the end of the Civil War, industrialization stimulated fresh hatreds and bloody clashes. Employers sent armies of spies and private detectives against budding trade unions. Organizers were murdered, meetings smashed and where these efforts failed, sympathetic government officials sent troops to break strikes. The media, newspapers, and magazines, portrayed unions as being run by cartoon-like, bomb-throwing aliens.

In the 1890s, bigots unleashed seething racial and religious hatreds. In the southeast, bloodthirsty mobs slew Blacks and in the southwest, Texas Rangers and Whites slew Chicanos. These murderers rarely faced juries—and some were lawmen. In New Orleans, a White mob besieged a jail and lynched Italian prisoners being held for trial.

A fanatically anti-Catholic American Protective Association lobbied for anti-foreign immigration laws, and promoted street violence. Its 70 weeklies and many books featured sensational Papal conspiracies— Lincoln's assassination was its favorite.

At the turn of the century, Senator Tom Watson of Georgia found rich rewards by creating scandalous Catholic and Jewish plots for his widely-read weekly, *The Jeffersonian*. By the 1920s, anti-Semitism had become so important to Henry Ford that his Dearborn *Independent* spent seven years and a fortune selling not only his Model A or T cars but "Jewish conspiracies."

These crusades demonstrated that Klan-type thinking had deep historic roots in American soil; they established that citizens would pay money to exercise their racial and religious hate. Last, they created a fertile soil for the seeds of a nationwide, grass-roots Invisible Empire with broad interests.

A new KKK gained impetus from American imperialist expansion. In 1898, a United States comfortably isolated from the world leaped into international leadership. "We must take Hawaii in the interests of the White race," announced Teddy Roosevelt as waves of enthusiasm swept the country. As empires of dark-skinned people fell under U.S. domination, Klan racial arguments became strong pillars of U.S. foreign policy.

The new Invisible Empire also built on fears created by chaotic and wrenching changes. A nation of small farmers and country ways was forced to retreat before giant puffing industries and huge crowded cities. Its Protestants who always had been a majority felt elbowed aside by millions of Catholic and Jewish immigrants. The ordinary citizen faced a bewildering array of fresh isms—unionism, communism, feminism, atheism, imperialism and militarism. Religion and traditional wisdom offered few insights into such volcanic eruptions.

Millions of citizens felt like frustrated passengers whose fast-moving train had just pulled out and left them muttering resentfully on the platform. They correctly sensed the future would be more of the same. The Klan played on their fears that world events were overtaking decent, God-fearing folks.

The revolutionary changes citizens faced—or refused to face—were real enough, but rarely vicious or violent. The new era was powered by a host of spectacular inventions—airplanes, telephones, radios, automobiles, movies (and talkies by 1927). These devices feverishly cruised the nation's spine: in seconds, they sent words or music over airwaves; in hours, they swept passengers across or over Continents; and they spun people on rubber wheels supplied by the Ford company.

Innovations transformed communities. An old America—with religion and country ways dominating life, men controlling women and children, the oppressed accepting a dreary lot—this America was taking its last gulp. Many swayed to the hypnotic rhythms of the new jazz. But others saw a safe world careen toward death's canyon with jazz musicians playing wildly in the background.

World War I hysteria had given birth to grave new dangers. Government officials were convinced that ruthless anti-German propaganda offensives were necessary to stimulate enlistments, sell bonds and raise civilian morale. U.S. information agencies used the media to force-feed the public dubious truths and spectacular lies.

German-Americans or people who spoke German were attacked by mobs. Three state governments and high schools from Maine to Oregon banned the teaching of German. In this hysteria over "Huns," sauerkraut was renamed "liberty cabbage."

But the publicity barrage was aimed at broader targets than blood-

Newspaper woman Ida B. Wells of Memphis, Tennessee, at 19 began the modern crusade against lynchings.

stained Germans. People who opposed US entrance into the war on religious, pacifist or political grounds suffered government prosecution and local fury. Called slackers, anarchists, subversives, enemy agents, or "Reds," these people found their loyalty doubted, their jobs and children in danger.

During the war, U.S. authorities began a frantic search for spies and saboteurs. The government net swept wide and Constitutional protections were conveniently forgotten. Anyone who opposed the war, the draft or the Allies could end up in prison. Some 867 Americans were jailed, and not one was a spy or saboteur. But this type of official witch-hunting shaped a climate that would nourish a renovated Invisible Empire.

Disillusionment and a search for scapegoats flowed from the frustrations of World War I. "The war to make the world safe for democracy" and "the war to end all wars," had ended in failure. Although the Allies had won, their peace treaty had economically stripped and psychologically humiliated the foe. This created fresh combustion for future wars.

After European royal families were executed or forced to flee, a new crop of tyrants seized power and prepared bigger, more lethal arsenals. The democratic spirit was not victorious, but in flight. Millions had died in vain and the agony of their loss mixed with a gloomy sense that little had changed.

This anguish produced either despair or workers' revolutions. In Russia, a vigorous new force called communism reigned and promised workers' management of the state. It marched on Parliaments in Hungary, Germany and Italy. A ruthless iron fist called Fascism in Italy and Nazism in Germany, pounded it down. Liking the use of its muscles, fascism stretched its fingers toward power. Its hallmarks were violence, super-patriotism and racism. Fascism united crooks and thieves under a strict military code that aimed to eliminate democracy and minorities.

This clash of baffling overseas forces magnified the fright and political chaos in the US. Voters rejected President Woodrow Wilson, war hero of the nation, and elected his Republican opponents. Confusion became deep dismay when Wilson suffered a massive stroke that left him too disabled to direct the affairs of state. The President's idealistic project, a League of Nations, was brushed aside by the US Senate.

Finally, in 1920, Republican Warren G. Harding, who promised a vague, calming "normalcy," won overwhelming election to the Presidency. Upon Harding's death in 1923, some of his Cabinet members were exposed for their corrupt use of high office.

The alarm over foreigners and the fear of a "Red Revolution" blossomed into a massive hunt for U.S. communists and radicals. Identifying and chasing "Reds" became a national obsession and an effort that attracted marketing and publicity experts.

Those who charged that Communists plotted to destroy democracy pointed to labor unrest. When 4 million women and men went on strike in 1919, "Reds" were blamed. When the Boston police struck, and law

In 1917 a "silent parade" was held by Blacks in New York City to protest mounting lynchings and Klan violence.

and order tottered, politicians spoke of a vast "Red" plot. When a laborers' committee ran Seattle during a city-wide strike, it was whispered that "Reds" were exporting insurrection. When a bomb exploded on Wall Street, financial capital of the country, and left 30 dead, citizens were asked to brace for revolutionary terror. Though nothing happened, fear of "Reds" became a permanent US house guest.

Attorney General A. Mitchell Palmer saw a chance to coast into the White House by manufacturing his own nationwide "Red Scare." On January 1, 1920, his FBI agents fanned out and arrested about 6,000 men and women whom Palmer claimed were "dangerous aliens." He held prisoners without bail and forcefully deported some 249 "undesirables" to the USSR. His swift action, he insisted, spiked a budding "Red" bloodbath.

In his bold stride toward the White House, Palmer echoed a popular line: "We must purify the sources of America's population." He also waved a super-patriot's banner: "I myself am an American and I love to preach my doctrine before 100% Americans because my platform is undiluted Americanism." Palmer's campaign collapsed, but hysteria remained strong.

Political turbulence had its counterpart in post-war economic life. Prices soared out of control and consumer goods became scarce. In 1919, a sharp depression lasting for a year crippled the country. Farmer's economic woes continued through the hard times of the 1930s. This was not the land of financial stability that peace had promised. For the ordinary citizen there were few heroes, nothing one could count on and little that turned out right. Clouds of suspicion and doubt billowed over the land.

Long term changes also baffled people. Stimulated by war needs, there had been a chaotic spurt of industrialization. Cities sprang up near factories. America was no longer a homespun nation of farmers and artisans. This was not the land of one's fathers and mothers. In 1920, for the first time in history, most Americans lived not in towns or on farms but in large cities.

Urban life excited, awed and panicked people. Millions of citizens had left their homes for dazzling urban skylines. Basically religious and rural in their ways, they were hardly prepared for its many risks or bold demands. Sitting in dark, narrow apartments, or walking streets teeming with strangers, they faced a spooky world. Temptation chipped away at their religious devotion and eroded their staunchly pious morality.

Protestants felt trembling in facing newcomers they had not seen before. Crowded ghettoes teemed with Catholic or Jewish immigrants talking strange languages. "The Kikes are so thick that a White man can hardly find room to walk on the sidewalk," said an Oregon man. For these Whites, the millions of Southern Blacks who migrated into run-down neighborhoods, also symbolized urban life's dangers and mysteries.

Perhaps worst of all, White Protestants faced an ambush from inside their families. Women who had worked during the war were not souls to be held down by religious strictures or rigid rules. The 19th Amendment granted women the right to vote and made them political equals, and this spurred the energetic to test themselves in more comfortable clothing, in jobs, in fresh situations and among new friends.

Though they loved them dearly, women began to reject cranky or

Government troops were sent to Chicago in 1919 when Blacks retaliated against armed Whites who invaded their neighborhoods.

domineering fathers or husbands. To many men, this sounded like a large mutiny aboard a small ship. They felt their previously uncontested stern hand over wives, sisters and daughters slapped or shoved away. Family arguments became more bitter and divorces more common.

For many Protestant newcomers, the thumping, erotic jazz music stood for the influences ripping families apart. One doctor claimed proof that jazz "causes drunkenness. . .and stronger animal passions." Crusaders in New York, Cleveland, Philadelphia, Kansas City and Detroit forced their city councils to prohibit jazz in public dance halls. The new Klan raised the cross of modern puritanism against sinful children and women.

Blacks, the traditional victims of the Klan, were causing new alarm. Whites dreaded that Black U.S. troops, who had risked death on European battlefields, might demand justice at home. They were right. Led by their ex-soldiers, Black Americans demonstrated a conviction that opportunities should not just apply to Whites. Led by Marcus Garvey, they spiritedly pushed for Black self-help, Black-run businesses and a "return to the ancestral home in Africa."

North and South, the White response to any Black agitation was violence. In 1919, 26 major U.S. cities—including Chicago and Washington, DC—exploded in riots. Armed White mobs surged into Black ghettoes. Unlike previous riots, these assaults found Blacks defending their homes with guns. When White casualties mounted, troops restored order. In the South, 76 Black Americans, some still in Army uniforms, were lynched.

By 1920, America's dazzling, faceless cities had acquired more crimes than they could handle. The 18th Amendment had banned the manufacture and sale of liquor and beer, and the casual act of sipping a beer became illegal. Crooks stepped in to run a lucrative liquor business, and their illegal "speakeasies" sold what people were willing to pay for. Chemists hired by criminals rarely produced good tasting or even safe beverages. Some customers became sick, and a few swallowed and died.

For a dozen years, cops and FBI agents shot it out in a fruitless war against crime. Ironically, more liquor was sold after than before Prohibition. As lawmen looked the other way, the booze kept floating toward cash-paying customers. The modern Klan would focus on crime in the streets, and immorality everywhere.

The Klan approach to the serious problems of the day was calculated to provide a home for confused, disillusioned, angry citizens with a nostalgia for easier days. It recruited from the most jittery, uncertain and prejudiced.

The new Invisible Empire stitched together a hate program inspired by earlier efforts. It built on doctrines molded by slaveholders, anti-

Black victims of the 1919 Chicago riot are led away by police.

union employers, the first Klan, the American Protective Association, Senator Tom Watson and inventor Henry Ford. Into this stew they poured the scorching malice and fury that had bubbled to the top with wartime hysteria.

This Klan fought for a puritanical, chaste world and "100% Americanism." "The great city," shouted one Imperial Wizard, "corrodes the very soul of American life." For Klansmen, the city meant nonconformists, Blacks, Catholics, Jews, people who did not speak English; a sexually suggestive jazz music; and independent women who saw life beyond home, family and church. Against this terrifying urban America, it strongly proclaimed the "God-fearing ways" of a Biblical Christianity.

71

In launching a new Invisible Empire, its organizers chose tested seeds and a fertile 1920s climate. Klan rhetoric whipped trembling and cold sweat into a blend that worked wonders during recruitment drives. In papering over issues with mindless phobias and plots, they created fresh problems or inflated old ones. Worse, they made solutions more distant.

The Twenties became bigotry's wildest American hayride. A reborn Ku Klux Klan soon had millions of US citizens in "the land of the free and the home of the brave" hiding behind masks.

8

"THE BIRTH
OF A NATION"

IN THE DECADES BETWEEN THE DEATH of one Klan and the rise of the new one, the bloody record of the first was conveniently white-washed. In the minds of new generations, their Klan ancestors had saved southern civilization.

Thomas Dixon, a young North Carolina writer and dramatist, was not the first southerner to mythologize the Klan into an order of noble, chivalrous knights. But his efforts proved the most effective. The rebirth of The Invisible Empire has forever been linked to his fertile imagination and steadfast purpose.

One of Dixon's earliest memories was as a child of five witnessing a Klan parade in the moonlight of his hometown of Shelby, North Carolina. When the boy became frightened by the silent robed horsemen riding, his mother comforted him by saying "They're our people—they're guarding us from harm."

Early in life Dixon became smitten by the "romance" of the Ku Klux Klan. He also grew up knowing his uncle, Colonel Leroy MacAfee, led the Invisible Empire in Piedmont. As a young man, Dixon harbored little racial animosity and believed equality of all people was a valued goal. At the turn of the century, his beliefs changed when U.S. troops were sent off to rule over dark-skinned people in the Caribbean and the Pacific. He began to accept and then defend ideas of racial purity and white power.

Dixon envisioned The Invisible Empire of reconstruction days as a heroic adventure, one that he promised to revive in the most dramatic forms he could find. For him, Klan raiders were not hooded marauders but gallant White knights who had saved southern civilization from African barbarism. To preserve his vision on a creative canvas became Dixon's goal in life.

A brilliant young man, Dixon graduated from college and was elected to the North Carolina legislature—before he was 21. A restless soul, he left politics for the Baptist ministry, left the pulpit to become a lecturer, and ended up writing romantic novels based on the "lost cause" of his "gallant South."

Dixon's cast of characters included noble White gentlemen and their fine ladies—and evil, treacherous Blacks intent on murder and rape. As this unreal, dreamy southland bewitched his imagination, he longed to write an epic tale that would grip audiences as never before.

His 1906 novel, THE CLANSMAN, AN HISTORICAL ROMANCE OF THE KU KLUX KLAN, aimed to do just that. Emerging from Dixon's pen, the Klan terrorists of the Reconstruction Era became masked saviors rescuing White maidens from a Black fate worse that death. A gushy love story about chaste White maidens and their male heroes knitted the novel's thin plot together.

The book soon became a play, with Dixon playing the lead. Then he decided that his drama should become part of that new art form, the moving picture, which was sweeping the nation. He searched for a movie director who shared his passion for the subject, and found D.W. Griffith. Impatient for a chance to showcase his sparkling talent, Griffith leaped at the opportunity.

In 1914, when the two met for the first time, movies were a nickel novelty, and ran for about thirty silent minutes. They had no plots to speak of, but merely demonstrated how a cameraman could capture people's actions, portray their emotions, and create exciting visual tricks. No one had yet thought of telling a detailed and important story through the camera's eye.

Griffith changed movies forever. With his cameraman, Billy Bitzer, he used Dixon's Klan romance to make screen history. The three men shaped Dixon's characters and dramatic plot into flickering images on a silver screen that had audiences gasping at the excitement. They named it *The Birth of A Nation*.

Crowds lined up to pay an unheard of $2 each, and in one city after another the film broke all previous attendance records. For almost three hours, audiences encountered characters they dearly loved or passionately hated. For most of that time, they were electrified by the tension leaping from the silver screen.

Scene from movie classic "The Birth of a Nation." (Museum of Modern Art/Film Stills Archives)

Griffith and Bitzer brought Dixon's novel to life with striking film techniques they invented and used for the first time. They cut dramatically from one scene to another, or moved swiftly from a panoramic shot to a close-up. The camera carefully picked up a tiny tear making its way down a sad face, then flew off to capture galloping horsemen riding to save humanity.

A special musical score, for an orchestra of 30, wove in classics, spirituals and patriotic themes. Viewers screeched and cried, and came back for more. Before the talkies arrived in 1927, 50 million Americans had seen it and made it a screen classic. It still breathes excitement and thrills.

Because the movie had a documentary look, people took it as historical truth. At the movie's climax, Klansmen raced their steeds to save little White Flora Cameron from a Black rapist. Audiences had been agitated to frenzy. As it never had been dramatized before, this was a confrontation between White good and Black evil that stirred every man, woman and child.

People not only believed everything they saw about the Ku Klux Klan, but they might have been ready to fight for the Klan on the screen or off, had they been asked. With that kind of stimulation, they left theaters and returned home to the reality of a multi-racial country.

A part of the historical record had been packaged in a form that reached and touched even those who paid no attention in their school history classes. *The Birth of A Nation* became a propaganda vehicle of staggering impact. Few who cheered the heroic masked horsemen knew that they had swallowed a savage distortion of the American past.

Scene from "The Birth of a Nation." (Museum of Modern Art/Film Stills Archive)

Some Black scholars challenged the movie's mangling of facts and its twisted interpretation of the Klan. However, the silent message from silver screen spoke more eloquently than all the critics. Besides, each attack only brought more White adults to see for themselves what the clamor was about.

To undercut his critics and gain national publicity for the film, Dixon contacted the White House and his old college friend, President Woodrow Wilson. During a special showing in the White House's East Room, the Virginia-born President and historian suddenly became animated and eloquent. He turned to Dixon, said his story was "terribly true" and exclaimed it was "history written in lightning." Dixon had the first film to bear a Presidential stamp of approval.

Encouraged, the next night Dixon showed his masterpiece before members of the Supreme Court and Congress. Again the approval was vocal and heartfelt. This time it provoked Chief Justice Edward White. He leaned over and proudly confided in Dixon's ear, "I was a member of the Klan, sir."

When THE BIRTH OF A NATION opened in Atlanta, Georgia, for an unprecedented three week run, next to its announcement in a local paper was an ad for a revived Ku Klux Klan. The person who placed the ad was William Simmons, a restless soul, unsuccessful at any kind of work, but a man who shared Dixon's romance with the old Klan.

Born on an Alabama farm to poor parents, Simmons had an illness at 20 that kept him in bed. His Klan fantasies danced imaginatively across his sick room wall. He wrote:

> On horseback in their white robes they rode across the wall in front of me. As the picture faded out I got down on my knees and swore I would found a fraternal organization that would be a memorial to the Ku Klux Klan.

Simmons served as a private in the Spanish-American War, then became a Methodist minister. His backwoods revival meetings had farm people under his spell shouting out their emotions. But the pay was low and Simmons sank into debt. To pay these debts, he was rumored to have sank his hand into other people's pockets. The Methodist leaders denied him a promotion, stating he was unreliable and immoral.

Simmons turned to salesmanship but left that to become an organizer of fraternal lodges then growing in popularity across the South. Like many American men, he enjoyed becoming a part of a friendly organization. "I am a fraternalist," he often said.

An accident changed his life. Struck down in Atlanta in 1911 by an automobile, he spent three months recovering. From his hospital bed, he carefully worked out a plan for "The Invisible Empire, Knights of the Ku Klux Klan." His choice of slogan emphasized charity: "Not for self, but for others." Simmons wisely copyrighted the organization's name, rituals and robes.

On Thanksgiving Eve, 1915, Simmons gathered his followers at the

Some early leaders of the "new" Invisible Empire gather for a member's wedding. (Library of Congress)

Atlanta Hotel and announced a surprise. He led 15 men onto a rented bus waiting outside the hotel and they drove 16 miles to Stone Mountain, a huge granite slab jutting into the sky. With their lights piercing the night darkness, they stumbled and climbed the stone trail, 1650 feet up to the mountain's top.

Lashed by wintry winds and freezing temperatures, Simmons and his men built an altar of stones. They erected a big wooden cross and placed a U.S. flag, a sword, an open Bible and a canteen nearby. Someone doused the cross with kerosene, threw in a lighted match—and flames illuminated the cold night sky. Simmons stepped forward and solemnly promised that a new Ku Klux Klan would "take up a new task and fulfill a new mission."

His new KKK utilized the old one's language. Its ritual was called a Kloran, officers were Kleagles, Kligrapps, Cyclops, Goblins, Kludds, and he was the Imperial Wizard. Simmons' new Invisible Empire began slowly and attracted little attention.

When the US entered World War I, it wrapped itself in the American flag and became, according to Simmons, "my wartime secret service."

Unpatriotic talk was "reported to me." The Klan's first public act was to break a shipyard strike by workers. It warned Blacks were "getting uppity." By Armistice Day, the new order had a few thousand members, advertised itself as "A HIGH CLASS ORDER OF THE HIGHEST CLASS," but had yet to attract anyone of importance to its folds.

Simmons added a few new banners next to the old Klan's White supremacy. His creed proudly called for a red-blooded, two-fisted "comprehensive Americanism"—against unions, foreigners, "Reds" and Jews. The list was hardly original, but Simmons was not seeking originality. On the contrary, if his secret order was to become a popular success, it required foes that everyone agreed upon.

All he needed now, Simmons concluded, was some spectacular advertising. In June, 1920, Simmons hired Edward Clarke and Bessie Tyler of the Southern Publicity Association. The moment was right, their salesmanship was on target and Protestants rushed for membership blanks. "The minute we said Ku Klux," Mrs. Tyler recalled, "editors from all over the United States began literally pressing us for publicity."

Promised four of every five dollars collected, the two agents labored diligently digging up recruits. They sent out 1,100 Kleagles (recruiters) across the country in "kluxing" or recruiting drives. In 16 months, 100,000 White Protestant men had each paid $10 to join the new Invisible Empire.

To insure the success of their campaign, Kleagles first approached Baptist and Methodist ministers and offered them free membership positions. Many became Kludds (or Chaplains) for Klan Klaverns (Dens). A Kleagle would be invited to address Sunday religious services, followed by the local minister urging his congregation to join "this good Christian society."

By September, 1921, Simmons now installed as Imperial Wizard, had earned $170,000, an additional $25,000 in back pay and had been granted a splendid $33,000 Klan home. His KKK was not only a sacred crusade, but a big business. Just a few years before, Simmons remembered, he had "walked the streets until my shoes wore through because I had no money." The Invisible Empire had a factory for making its regalia, one for printing Klan propaganda and a real estate company to manage its properties.

The Klan's success rested on its splashy, spectacular advertising campaigns. Particularly helpful had been the movie *THE BIRTH OF A NATION*. The earlier Klan's shocking criminal record, its rampant bigotry and its violent effort to overthrow state governments established by the United States Congress were distant, forgotten memories.

In the process of constructing his organization, Simmons learned something the first Klan knew—that a touch of violence appeals to many men. During a Georgia meeting, he took a revolver from one pocket and a Colt automatic from another and placed them dramatically on a table. Then he draped his cartridge belt between the two weapons, and said "Now let the Niggers, Catholics, Jews and all others who disdain my imperial wizardry, come on." This was a safe dare, since he knew that none of these minorities would be present in his audience.

Thomas Dixon and D. W. Griffith watched the human stampede to the banner of a new Ku Klux Klan, and both had second thoughts. A reporter asked Dixon what he thought of the new secret order and his answer was short—"stupid and inhuman."

D. W. Griffith gave his response by directing a silent movie spectacular called *INTOLERANCE*. It portrayed the cruel tortures and mass murders carried forth throughout history by those who persecuted others.

Dixon and Griffith had learned fast. Klansmen learned slowly.

9

THE FASTEST GROWING
CLUB IN AMERICA

THE FIRST INVISIBLE EMPIRE TRIED TO grind down Black hopes, drive Yankees from the South and fashion a return to slavery. The second KKK attacked many foes on a broader front, and in a new search for victims, reached far beyond Black communities. Shouting "Americanize America," it spread to 48 states.

Klan recruiting success stemmed from its ability to touch millions of Protestants with the harrowing message that they were "constantly discriminated against" and faced overwhelming perils. Grand Goblin F.W. Watkins warned followers to "protect our homes, our lives, our people and our nation's future against a wave of living hell." A Klan speaker struck a responsive chord when he claimed "The Nordic American today is a stranger in a large part of the land his fathers gave him."

White supremacy alone could hardly captivate millions. But Klan publicity was able to persuade millions of White citizens that massive terror threatened United States citizens from Communism in the USSR, the Pope in Rome, strikes and unions, Blacks and foreigners in cities, modern women, and mortal sin everywhere. This Invisible Empire directed its propaganda at what it might have called a Protestant "moral majority."

A modern breed of Klan organizer discovered there was ready money to be squeezed from terrified people. In return for cowering scapegoats, quick answers, and some exciting night action, men would hand over their hard-earned cash. Strumming the resonant chords of anxiety and arrogance in people, their bluff stampeded millions and built rewarding financial empires.

The 1920s was the first great decade of American advertising, and the Klan relied on its persuasive techniques. Klan parades, night initiation ceremonies, street brawls and cross burnings were hot copy. "We have been given fifty million dollars worth of free advertising by the newspapers," smiled an Imperial Wizard.

In the early days, even bad publicity helped stimulate membership. The New York *World* ran a three-week expose of KKK violence, extortion and terror that was syndicated in 18 US newspapers. It sold papers, and attracted eager recruits.

Then the US Congress investigated The Invisible Empire. When it summoned William Simmons, the tall, elegantly-dressed Imperial Wizard foiled their plans. He looked more like a kindly uncle who would give children candy and good advice about life than the director of a private army. He swore the KKK never engaged in violence, always obeyed the Constitution and laws, and stood for "straight Americanism." He appeared charming.

With a haughty eloquence and some big lies, Simmons spent three days defending his Klan. He wound up a hero and later credited the Congressional hearings with spurring Klan growth:

> Congress gave us the best advertising we ever got. Congress made us.

Klan propaganda focused on two popular issues. The first was a world-wide, alleged Catholic conspiracy directed from the Vatican. It was aimed at undermining the public schools and democracy. Some Protestants were willing to believe that President Wilson and other officials had become "tools of the Papacy." Something had to be done. In 1920, a Klan Methodist minister shot a Catholic priest to death on his doorstep, and in Illinois two hours after a Klan meeting, a Catholic church was burned to the ground.

The second issue the Klan harped on was mounting lawlessness in cities, and Klansmen became self-appointed leaders of a crusade for Christian and family values. Announced a New York City Klavern, The Invisible Empire had arrived "to represent the decent, God-fearing, law-abiding vote."

Local officials, shocked at the rise in crime, were attracted by this talk. Governor Pat Neff of Texas declared "Murder, theft, robbery and hold-ups are hourly occurrences." He blamed corrupt public officials: "Our loose method of dealing with violators of the law is in a large degree responsible for the conditions that today confront us." The Tulsa

Klan march in Washington, DC during the 1920s. (Library of Congress)

Tribune agreed: "Our jails are sieves and at times our courts appear to be a joke." In words echoing the Klan approach, Governor Neff said the battle was "clearly drawn. . .between law and lawlessness, between virtue and vice, between social order and open violence."

Klansmen rode into towns, said an Oklahoma recruit, to chase out "the gangster, bootlegger, chock [beer] shop, fast and loose females, and the man who abuses and neglects his wife and children." For Klansmen, personal family problems, criminal behavior, non-Christian religions, all could be traced to foreign intrigues. The Invisible Empire recruited heavily from those who took conspiracy theories to heart.

Klan speakers linked common problems or fears to one or several ghostly forces. The more remote the foe, the easier to accuse it of diabolical plots. Grand Goblin F.W. Atkins shouted to his gullible followers that their choice was between "real Americansim" and "the devil's scheme."

Klan speakers claimed foes were ready to unleash terrifying destruction. "The Negro," claimed Klan lecturer R.H. Sawyer, "is more dangerous than a maddened wild beast." "Aliens" said another lecturer, "were the most dangerous of all invaders."

Initiation ceremonies combined drama, fright, and a sense of belonging. Recruits swore to uphold the secrets of the Klan until death. This Klan gathering took place in Illinois in the 1920s. (Library of Congress)

For Klansmen, "Aliens" meant anyone outside their trusted circle. Subversive influences were at work when women smoked in public, wore their hair short, or danced to jazz music. Alien ideas encouraged teen-agers to disobey their fathers, not attend church, and pet in parked cars.

Hundreds, sometimes thousands of men knelt before flaming crosses during awesome night meetings. They were told "the rich, red blood of American patriots and martyrs runs through your veins." In remote fields, as huge crosses crackled in the night air, they solemnly promised their lives to the KKK.

They began the ceremony as store clerks, high school drop-outs, accountants, policemen or mechanics. But in that eerie light and the strange shadows cast by a burning cross, these vulnerable, sometimes misfit men were transformed. They became guardians of The Flag and "the sacredness of chastity."

Dull, drab lives, enlisted for a crusade against "the godless home," were rocked into heavens of excitement. They had joined a growing fraternity of men like themselves who pledged to stand shoulder to brave shoulder against a monster who prowled the earth in human form.

Members of The Invisible Empire soon lurched forward on strange assignments. Reported one eyewitness "The Klan seemed to be watching everybody." In Portland, Oregon, two Klansmen branded a woman on her chest. Now, announced one, "she won't wear any more low-necked dresses." Waving whip and fire, the Klan made itself the moral police force of a nation.

Klan halls had an altar and a US flag, and meetings opened and closed with a prayer. "The living Christ is a Klansman's criterion of character," announced one Klan minister. The southern rural Baptist and Methodist clergy, except in Virginia and North Carolina, joined or worked with the Klan. Many became leaders. A Klan presence in a community was often first announced when the hooded order appeared at Sunday worship services. Robed figures marched to the altar and made a cash donation. Some members carried holiday food packages to the needy.

Having offered themselves as Christian soldiers fighting the forces of evil that would rule the world, Klansmen stressed the jolting power of the alien foe. Imperial Wizard Simmons warned repeatedly that aliens might "crush and overwhelm Anglo-Saxon civilization." He spoke of deadly peril:

> The dangers were in the tremendous influx of foreign immigration, tutored in alien dogmas and alien creeds, flowing in from all climes and slowly pushing the native-born white American population to the center of the country, there to be ultimately overwhelmed and smothered.

Imperial Wizard Hiram Evans told what aliens had "torn away" from good Protestants:

> We found our great cities and the control of much of our industry and commerce taken over by strangers who stacked the cards of success against us.

In addition to its effective manipulation of the emotions of jealousy and hate, Klansmen built on the US male's need to belong. A large amount of Klan success lay in its creation of a club where Protestants found fellowship with their "own kind." Men clustered tightly in The Invisible Empire's clubs, drinking beer, slapping backs and swapping jokes. Within the mysterious, hidden confines of their secret order, they could feel comfort, security and "Klanishness."

Klan recruiters initially aimed to sign up a community's ministers and business people. Armed with some prestigious names, they attracted others. Many—particularly lawmen and firemen—joined to combat the rising corruption in U.S. society.

For merchants and professionals, the KKK became good business and a source of new customers. The Invisible Empire found it was not always useful to remain invisible, and Klan merchants sponsored TWAK (Trade With A Klansman) campaigns.

Members joined for their own reasons. Some signed up because they felt they would lose out financially by remaining outside. Some felt safer from harm inside than out. Politicians joined, hoping to recruit campaign workers and gather more votes at election time.

For some, the Klan was a chance to commit crimes or ignite a violent fuse. For others who stumbled in, it was a rare chance to feel superior by brutalizing helpless victims. For leaders, the KKK often was a lucrative enterprise.

For many members, it filled a great need to belong, to be with others who shared their view of a world spinning helplessly out of control. It appeared in the early 1920s that just about every male, red-blooded Protestant was joining.

The Invisible Empire cost so little—$10 to sign up and $6 more for a gown and hood. Each week, from Maine to Florida, from New York to California, from Minnesota to Texas, members and their dollars rolled in by the hundreds and thousands.

How did members square the Klan's patriotism with its racial and religious animosity? In the 1920s, White Christians justified rather than apologized for fears of and fury against nonwhites. Racism enjoyed widespread popular support. Prominent citizens aimed irresponsible, damning charges at minorities.

The KKK used pageantry and school children to attract new members. This Texas den prepared a play, "The Awakening," in 1924 to demonstrate the virtues of the Invisible Empire.

Warren G. Harding warned the public about "racial differences" and said immigration should only be permitted for those with a "full consecration to American practices and ideals." Calvin Coolidge wrote that "biological laws show us that Nordics deteriorate when mixed with other races." Herbert Hoover said recent immigrants to America "would be tolerated only if they behaved." During the decade of the Twenties, each of these men served as a President of the United States.

Klaverns were named after Presidents Harding and Coolidge and Klansmen winked that they "had a friend in the White House." In Missouri, a young (and future President) Harry Truman joined and in Alabama, a young (and future Supreme Court Justice) Hugo L. Black enrolled. Some members claimed that in the 1920s at least one President had become a Klansman, but no concrete evidence was offered to substantiate this.

Ordinary Klan members might swallow almost anything their leaders said, and their imaginations could be guided into bizarre actions. A Klan lecturer in Indiana roused his audience to a fever by insisting "The

Pope may even be on the northbound train tomorrow. He may. He may." The next afternoon a thousand wild citizens rushed to the depot ready to battle the Pope. The only descending passenger from the northbound train proved to be a salesman. He had a hard time convincing the milling crowd that he was not the Pope in disguise, just someone trying to sell men's underwear.

For men who travelled from one lonely city or town to another in their work, there was an additional incentive for taking out a membership. Far from home, they might find a warm hand of friendship or a drinking partner they could trust.

In a strange city, a visiting member of The Invisible Empire could amble up to a bar and ask "A Y A K?" Someone would answer "A K I A." To the question "Are You A Klansman?" a lonely traveller had heard the comforting news "A Klansman I Am."

The secret order wrapped an insecure man in warm fellowship, and surrounded him with friends. He was not just another lost soul, but part of a powerful, patriotic Invisible Empire with branches everywhere. All stood prepared, in the words of a New York City Klavern minister, "to resist the corruption of politics, the lawlessness of our times."

In its first decade, millions joined the new Ku Klux Klan—estimates range from three to five million. One authority has said that one in every four Protestants joined. Such a muscular, dynamic American force could not long be ignored.

10

KLAN WARS
IN THE STREETS

THE FIRST INVISIBLE EMPIRE RACED FAST horses over deserted southern roads and terrorized rural folks. The second Klan sputtered in second-hand cars across paved highways and clattered into American cities. Then Klansmen stepped down from their running boards and announced a war against "lawbreakers, crooks, and corrupt politicians." They remained to break the law and become corrupt.

The Klan proved strongest where city populations had grown the fastest. Between 1910 and 1920, urban populations soared in the south-west states of Oklahoma (68%), Texas (61%) and Arkansas (43%). The Invisible Empire dominated every city. Dallas was a KKK center and along its nearby Trinity river bottom, Klansmen kept a "whipping meadow" where dozens and dozens of men and women were kidnapped and lashed.

While Klan diatribes in Texas focused on minorities, it was fellow Protestants whose behavior was investigated and who felt the pain. "If we had a report about a man's immoral conduct we would. . .watch him from day to day and night to night to render reports," said a Waco Klansman. They listened in on phone calls, private conversations over coffee, and read personal mail.

Klaverns sent snoopers after people who wore "modern dress," danced to jazz music, and parked their cars for romance. One Dallas woman was stripped naked, tarred-and-feathered, and whipped for remarrying too soon after a divorce. Other Klan victims included a Black dentist, a man who spoke German, a doctor who performed abortions, a divorced Protestant man, and a White attorney with Black clients.

Klan raiders broke a strike of Black cotton field laborers and routinely terrorized major Black communities. Over 500 Texans suffered humiliations ranging from brandings to lynchings.

In Oklahoma, where one in every 20 citizens had joined their Governor in the hooded order, the state's Grand Wizard was the Vice President of the University of Oklahoma. In 1923, Klan raiders whipped 2,300 men and women. They also found time to stop cars at night and send home unmarried couples. They beat a man who took money from his sister-in-law and another who argued with his wife. In Enid, Klansmen decided who would be allowed to join the Enid Musical Society. Enid's Mayor said "Our watchword is 'Keep your mouth shut and keep out of the hands of the Klansmen.' "

In the southwest, the Klan claimed its goal was "to enforce the 10 Commandments" and punish "wife-beaters," "family-deserters," and "home-wreckers." In Tulsa, "red-blooded, two-fisted" Klan members drove out corrupt Democrats and elected corrupt Republicans.

In the Ozarks, the hooded order rode out to break strikes, crush unions, and terrorize union organizers. Klansmen managed to shoot their way into a railroad strike and lynch a union man. They captured strikers, dragged them before a court of 12 Klansmen and sentenced them to gather up families and belongings and leave town. Klansmen forced the city council of Harrison to resign.

Southern Klansmen terrorized Black communities, but aimed their biggest guns at fellow White Protestants. In Louisiana, warfare left half a dozen dead and a thousand wounded as pro- and anti-Klan forces clashed, and Klansmen shot it out with rival Klansmen. Governor John Parker pleaded in vain for Federal military intervention to halt the massacres.

In Georgia, Blacks were beaten, Lebanese and Syrians driven from the state, and Catholic and Jewish businesses boycotted. Yet it was Protestants who took the most consistent blows. Protestant women were whipped for "immorality," "failure to attend church" or "abortion."

In Crenshaw, Alabama, a divorced farmer and his divorced wife were whipped together—in front of their children. The Klan clergyman who directed the lashing lectured the woman that his aim was "to show your children how a good mother should act." He handed the victim some Vaseline for her wounds, and left.

The first Invisible Empire remained below the Mason-Dixon line, but the second noisily roared into northern cities. It found a warm welcome. The Klan capitals of America were Indianapolis, Dayton, Dallas,

Each time a Black person was lynched, the NAACP office in New York City flew this flag from its window. The sign reads, "A man was lynched yesterday."

Portland (Oregon and Maine), Youngstown, and Denver. Chicago's 50,000 members and 20 huge Klaverns made it the largest Klan city. Detroit, Los Angeles, Philadelphia, and Pittsburgh had large Klaverns and many recruits. Even New York City, which Imperial Wizard Simmons called "the most un-American city of the American continent," had 21 Klaverns active in Manhattan, Brooklyn, and the Bronx.

California Klaverns attracted politicians, sheriffs, ministers, businessmen, and public workers. One night a prominent doctor who planned to divorce his wife was kidnapped by Klansmen, taken to a ball park, and stripped naked. With a crowd of leading citizens watching, he was beaten unconscious three times, and told to halt divorce proceedings. One California Grand Jury found that Klan actions were really motivated by "domestic troubles, jealousies, and other evidence of malice and hate."

Such evidence continued to pour in from around the country. Political intimidation and simple bigotry played a minor role as Klaverns tried to direct, discipline or alter the private lives of ordinary citizens. In Kansas, for example, Klansmen charged into homes in Emporia on

Sundays to make sure no one was playing cards. Elsewhere northern Klansmen interfered in family matters, told women the kinds of clothes they should wear, warned teen-agers to obey their parents, and instructed young and old to attend church regularly, and to love their country.

Ohio had such huge Klavern it could do little more than collect dues and hold giant meetings. In Illinois, Klansmen staged huge night initiations that inducted thousands of men into The Invisible Empire. One August night in Chicago a record 4,650 were initiated as 25,000 watched.

The Klan soon had its gallant heroes. With an automatic on each hip and a machine gun in his hands, Glen Young became the striking Klan figure in Illinois. He and his uniformed troops pushed into homes and businesses searching for criminals or immoral men and women. When finally brought to trial, Young and his soldiers arrived at the courthouse with guns drawn. A timid judge quickly acquitted them.

Encouraged in his criminal bravado, Young began a small war against the legal authorities in Williamson, and soon 20 men died fighting for or against him. When the sheriff hired a crack shot, Young decided to shoot it out with the sharpshooter. Both men died in a hail of bullets. Ministers eulogized Young as a Christian knight, and 40,000 followers attended his funeral. Williamson became quiet again.

$$* \quad * \quad * \quad * \quad *$$

In most Klan parades, someone carried a sign designed to calm those who had feared that The Invisible Empire meant trouble. The sign usually read "Decent People Have No Fear." But people soon began combatting the KKK in one town and city after another, often with furious Protestants taking the lead.

In Chicago, a weekly magazine, *Tolerance,* published by Catholics with Protestant, Jewish and Black support, struck at The Invisible Empire by printing thousands of members' names and calling for a boycott of Klan-run businesses. It was so effective, Klan spies infiltrated its ranks and tried to disrupt its activities.

In 1918, the NAACP hired Walter White, a blond, blue-eyed, quiet 25-year old, to expose racial violence. Despite his appearance, White was a tough Black man willing to go anywhere. For the next decade, he secretly entered Klan ranks and heard men confess their part in tortures and lynchings. Though his own life was in danger, he investigated 8 anti-Black riots and 41 lynchings, and devoted his life to the fight against mob violence.

The Klan's violence and arrogant interference in private lives also infuriated Whites. Some became steaming mad that anyone dared sit in judgment on their religion, behavior, manner of dress, or personal

Walter White, investigator for the NAACP, infiltrated the KKK. (Library of Congress)

habits. They were ready to fight over the hooded order's nerve in imposing morals, or questioning anyone's choice of friends or Saturday night fun. They scrawled a line in the dirt, and stood prepared to fight if it was crossed.

From fist fights to shoot-outs to full scale urban upheavals, spontaneous riots shattered the American night air. Klansmen announced a march or cross-burning, then armed and went off seeking trouble. Klan leaders believed a baptism of fire would demonstrate their great valor and pull in new members.

Beginning in 1922, cities from Laredo, Texas, to Framingham, Massachusetts, and west to Corning, Iowa, and Condon, Oregon, became battlefields. They echoed with the sound, fury and casualties of land warfare and in one a Klan plane was shot down.

Even in the South, citizen outrage boiled over. Citizens of Dallas, Texas, formed an anti-KKK league. Incendiaries set a Klan auditorium ablaze in Fort Worth, but failed in an effort to burn down its Beethoven Hall in San Antonio. Texas became the first of many states to pass "anti-mask" laws aimed at Klansmen.

In Missouri, Kansas City, residents bombed a hotel used by the Klan and threw bricks through a window featuring a KKK display. In Delaware, cross-burning near New Castle turned into a riot. Citizens shouted "To Hell with the Klan!" and "Hurrah for the Irish!" and charged into assembled Klansmen. Three died and 50 were wounded. Rioters in a Baltimore suburb attacked an anti-Catholic Klan meeting held in a church.

The Invisible Empire encountered stiffer resistance in the Midwest. At Niles, Ohio, citizens formed vigilante patrols to fight the hooded order. They searched cars arriving for a Klan meeting, tried to rip robes off members and began bashing faces and firing guns. It took machine-gun armed state troopers to restore order in Niles. In Steubenville, irate local citizens pulled arriving Klansmen from their cars and punched them.

Pennsylvania exploded with Klan disturbances. In Carnegie, the mayor banned a KKK march, but an Imperial Wizard ordered his forces forward into town. Bricks and bottles met the parade, then a mob of union men armed with clubs attacked the lines of hooded marchers. When a bullet slew one, the others fled. The mayhem continued the next week in Scottdale and Lilly, with rifle fire leaving four dead.

Hoping the worst was over, The Invisible Empire marched its forces into New Jersey. It guessed wrong. New Jersey resistance to the Invisible Empire was even stronger and sometimes united Blacks and Whites. Mayors called meetings to enlist "decent citizens" to keep the Klan out, and ministers of three faiths publicly united to denounce The Invisible Empire.

Citizens in Perth Amboy began by protesting a meeting and ended by fighting a small war. When Klansmen gathered at the Odd Fellow's Hall, local Catholic and Jewish leaders, backed by 3,000 noisy followers,

Black protest against lynchings and Klan activities never ceased during the height of Klan power. This demonstration in Washington, DC took place in June, 1922.

demanded entrance. When the police refused this request, the crowd swelled to 6,000.

A *New York Times* reporter on the scene thought it was "as if some secret call for reinforcements had been sent over the city." When the crowd became unruly, both police and fire departments were summoned. But now a full-scale riot was in progress. The mob surged through town. They cut fire hoses and sent the firemen home to bed.

Only the police remained to save shaking Klansmen from the wrath of Perth Amboy. Calm did not return until the next day when the State Militia arrived to disperse the mob. They rescued and escorted the Klansmen from town.

On September 1, 1923, a *New York Times* editorial noted the mounting anti-Klan violence: "At Steubenville, Binghamton, Pittsburgh and Perth Amboy there has been rioting of a grave character in which parading Klansmen have been stoned and beaten."

As disorder spread by 1924 and 1925 to New England, Massachusetts' cities became engulfed in anti-Klan strife. In Lancaster, hundreds of citizens besieged 200 Klan members whom police had to rescue. In Groveland the next night, three men were sent to the hospital for treatment of buckshot wounds and 21 others were jailed for rioting. Two days later a Shrewsbury shoot-out was interrupted when police and state troopers stepped in and disarmed both sides. In Worcester, 10,000 Klan members arrived for a daytime gathering, only to be stoned by a mob and to see their plane knocked out of the sky by anti-Klan rifle fire.

In 1925, other Massachusetts citizens attacked meetings of The Invisible Empire in Northbridge, Berlin, Gardner, Burlington, Westwood, Framingham, Reading, and North Brookfield. Residents armed with rocks and clubs, and sometimes guns and bullets, drove the hooded order out of their communities. These wild resisting forces usually welcomed a wide array of Klan targets and victims—from immigrant Catholics and union members to Protestants who thought the Klan had to be taught a lesson.

Sporadic warfare greeted other Klan rallies and parades. The first open Klan meeting in Corning, Iowa, in July, 1926, brought out residents armed with pitchforks, hammers and crowbars. They deployed in military fashion and turned back anyone who looked like a Klansman. A threat to summon troops finally sent people home.

As a violent organization, the Klan first welcomed these outbursts as baptisms of fire that would demonstrate their toughness. But something else was demonstrated in the fields, streets, and alleys of Middle America. Almost always these brawls pitted members against—not aliens—but decent (and militant) fellow Protestants.

Klansmen were seen to bring not Christianity but disorder. Towns and streets were peaceful until Klansmen arrived. To be fair, local people and their lawmen, even when they knew their own fathers and sons had started or shared in the trouble, routinely blamed The Invisible Empire.

One result of the bloody street rioting was preventative legislation. Throughout the Twenties scores of towns and cities, and the states of Iowa, Michigan, Minnesota and even Louisiana, passed laws against the public wearing of masks. Some local governments outlawed organizations with secret membership lists. To combat the Klan, Oklahoma's Governor first put Tulsa and then the entire state under martial law.

Police, mayors and judges cracked down on Klan lawlessness, and local authorities began to question the Klan's right to disturb communities. Increasingly states and municipalities, under pressure from the grass roots, denied The Invisible Empire marching or speaking permits or access to parks or public halls. One Grand Titan claimed that a Klansman "lives his life in the clear blue air of devotion to his country and its government." But each day fewer and fewer citizens believed this.

11

MASKED DEMOCRATS
AND REPUBLICANS

NO ONE WATCHED THE MARCHING FEET of the hooded order more closely than politicians. Even if The Invisible Empire's claim of five or six million members and twice that many voters was exaggerated, many had donned white gowns and hoods. The new secret order immediately leaped the boundaries of the first Klan.

By the elections of 1922 and 1924, politicians in many northern districts figured it was almost impossible to get nominated or elected if they faced Klan opposition. They may have been right.

Governors, Senators, and Congressmen who had once denounced the hooded order, now became quiet when the subject came up. A typical politician explained that the Klan "is nothing to joke about .... There are thousands of those fellows in my district." No, he would not give "an opinion about them."

After the congressional elections of 1922, the Klan had friends inside of both major parties and claimed 75 Congressmen. It helped elect Governors in Georgia, Alabama, California, and Oregon, and its three most popular lecturers were Senators Heflin of Alabama, Brewster of Maine, and Mayfield of Texas. The Klan opened headquarters on Washington, D.C.'s Massachusetts Avenue and began to receive some renowned visitors.

In Oregon, where they controlled the state apparatus, the Governor and the Mayor of Portland attended a Klan dinner and the Governor spoke on "Americanism." The Klan picked the president of the Senate and Speaker of the House in Oregon. In Colorado, The Invisible Empire controlled the Republican party, elected Governor Clarence Morely and two Senators, swept local and state elections, and ran the city of Denver.

In August, 1924, pro-KKK sentiment surprised everyone at both major party conventions. Both parties voted down resolutions that condemned the Ku Klux Klan by name. With about 300 Klan delegates from

Women and youth were a vital part of Black protests.

Kansas, Oklahoma, Iowa, Arkansas, Texas, and a score of other states, the Democratic National Convention met during the sweltering New York City summer.

For more than three days, The Invisible Empire was the main issue, and fist fights broke out in the Colorado and Missouri delegations. By only a few votes, a resolution calling the Klan Un-American was voted down. Klan leaders also insisted their delegates kept Al Smith, a Catholic, from receiving the party's nomination for President.

In the November elections, Klan-backed candidates not only held their 1922 ground but gained key Senate and Governorship seats in Indiana, Illinois, Colorado, Oklahoma, Kansas, and Kentucky. Hundreds of local offices throughout the country fell to candidates supported by The Invisible Empire.

At this point, it appeared that The Invisible Empire was destined to become the most influential force in US political life. It merely needed an attractive candidate to lead it down Washington's Pennsylvania Avenue and into the White House.

Some thought it had just that person in David Stephenson, the dynamic head of the huge Indiana KKK. He had dropped out of school after the sixth grade, moved from one job to another and learned that a young man could rise far by dressing well and understanding the psychology of people.

Stephenson's staff recruited a quarter of a million people and built a tight, state Klan network in Indiana. The dynamic young man was rewarded with control of 23 KKK state organizations. Handsome, charming, effective, Stephenson seemed headed for higher places, perhaps the White House.

"I am the law in Indiana," he shamelessly announced from his Indianapolis office. He had bodyguards to protect him, a bust of Napoleon to inspire him, and books on salesmanship and psychology to guide him. His own "Horse Thief Detective Associaiton"—a private police force—terrorized and ran the state. Bill Wilson, 18, remembered them well:

> They tarred and feathered drunks. They raided stills and
> burned barns. They caught couples in parked cars and tried to
> blackmail the girls or worse.

For months, each time Wilson came to pick up his girl by car, they trailed them. Wilson's father was a Congressman up for re-election, and he had defied Klan coercion to enroll him.

As election neared, the family received obscene phone calls, "KKK" was soaped on their window screens and their phone rang all night long. Congressman Wilson was finally defeated by the Klan, and lost again two years later.

In addition to keeping the pressure on uncooperative families like the Wilsons, Stephenson had 20,000 Klansmen deputized. They were permitted to carry weapons and detain suspects without warrants. They pushed into people's homes, cars and private lives. On election day, they intimidated the opposition.

In 1923, Klan members and supporters assembled 100,000 strong for Stephenson's coronation as Grand Dragon of the state. The star arrived late but stepped dramatically from his own plane with an explanation. He would have been on time but President Coolidge had kept him on important matters. It seemed nothing could stop Stephenson now.

But the rising star of The Invisible Empire was doomed to be brought down by his own hand. Stephenson, with his own yacht on Lake Michigan, private railroad car and plane, was pursued by many women. But his choice was Madge Oberholtzer, an Indiana public clerk. To protect her specific job as a clerk, he had the Indiana legislature amend one of its laws.

Although Stephenson wanted to marry her, Miss Oberholtzer had never encouraged this interest. One night he sent his bodyguards to bring her to his railroad car. There Stephenson raped her, announced she must marry him and said he would hold her prisoner until she agreed. She told him she had no intention of ever marrying him, and the next day escaped to a store where she bought and swallowed poison.

Sick and frightened, she returned to him to ask for help. Perhaps she felt this desperate act would soften his heart. She was mistaken. When she told Stephenson about the poison, he agreed to take her to a hospital—but only if she married him. No, was still her stubborn answer, and for a critical two days, Madge Oberholtzer was denied medical care. A week and a half later, after she told witnesses of Stephenson's refusal to take her for medical aid, she died.

In this case, even the Grand Dragon of Indiana could not stay the hand of Indiana justice. He was arrested and charged with second-degree murder, found guilty and sentenced to the Michigan City jail. He was confident his good friend, the Governor, whom he had placed in power, would pardon him. Nothing happened. His murder of an innocent woman had made the front pages and had lost him crucial support.

In 1925, at 36, David Stephenson sat not in the White House but in a jail cell. When the help he expected never arrived, he began to reveal letters and records from top politicians who received from or gave him money. When the Governor explained that a Stephenson check to him was for a horse that choked to death on a corn cob, the public choked with laughter.

Prison doors did not open for Stephenson until 1950, when he was finally placed on parole. He fled, was recaptured for parole violation and returned to jail. In 1956, he was finally released and quickly dis-

Women's units became a crucial part of the new Invisible Empire of the 1920's.

appeared into a world that no longer remembered the dynamic Klansman who would be President of the United States.

Like Stephenson, The Invisible Empire seemed to be coasting toward political success on a national scale. Like Stephenson, it shot itself in the foot, but over a longer period of time. Like Stephenson, the Klan was headed not up the mountains of political success but down into dank prison cells and disgrace.

The KKK began slipping in public esteem by the mid-1920s. One could tell the difference in their parades in the nation's capital in 1925 and 1926. In 1925, The Invisible Empire assembled an impressive 40,000 robed men and women to march down Pennsylvania Avenue in Washington, D.C.

A dozen bands enlivened the day with stirring music, and marchers gave Mussolini's Fascist, arms-raised, palms-down salute. Although a Klan speaker at the Washington Monument proclaimed "It won't rain! God won't let it"—the heavens opened up and Klan members, friends and families were drenched.

In 1926, the uniforms were more splendid and more women and girls marched than before. Blackshirts and brownshirts modeled after

Hitler's and Mussolini's forces stood out. An attractive "Miss America" rode on a float holding an open Bible.

The Imperial Wizard thundered for "aggressive warfare against Romanism, alienism, Bolshevism, and anti-Americanism of all kinds." But the 1926 parade was a disappointment—it had half the marchers of the previous year.

Klan popularity continued to sink, and in the 1926 elections, The Invisible Empire lost the spectacular ground it had gained in 1922 and 1924. Now candidates questioned its political clout.

To increase its membership, the Klan broke tradition with its predecessor of the Reconstruction era. The Twenties' Invisible Empire opened its doors wide to women. Enfranchised by the 19th Constitutional Amendment in 1919, they represented a huge electoral bloc. Besides, their membership dues and labor were highly appreciated.

Women were welcomed in separate units called "The Women of the Klan." In some larger industrial states, they equaled men in numbers. But their position was hardly equal to men. Kept to a subordinate status and roles in social events, they were excluded from the nasty "man's work" of terrorism.

Although Klan women, including the wives of Kleagles, had to fight off innumerable instances of sexual harassment, that was not their main problem. The women's units presented another vast cash crop Klansmen sought to manipulate. Many Kleagles appointed their wives as directors, the better to seize women's treasuries. Klan women fought back against these robberies as best they could, sometimes bringing cases to court.

During one female mutiny, Imperial Wizard Evans suspended the charters of seven Klaverns and warned both sides to cease and desist. Few took his advice. Soon Evans was back in court fighting discharged Pennsylvania members, and they rallied and counterattacked with proof of Klan violence, corruption and crimes. Evans lost.

The real loser each time was the carefully-crafted, shining image of the gallant knights of The Invisible Empire. The early gloss of Christian righteousness soon rubbed off the robed saviors and revealed the tarnish of deep corruption. These self-inflicted wounds deflated the reputation of the secret order, undermined its recruitment efforts and cost it victories at the polls.

In the 1928 election, the Klan tried to sail back into popularity by engineering the defeat of Al Smith, a Catholic, as the Democratic nominee for President. This was a last opportunity to regain important lost ground, and The Invisible Empire labored hard to bring about a resurgence.

The Invisible Empire wheeled out its biggest guns for the campaign. Senator Heflin toured meetings that paid his $150 to $200 fees predicting the Klan would stop the nomination. Despite Klan efforts and strong southern Protestant resentment over his religion, Smith was nominated. He became the first Catholic Presidential candidate selected by a major party.

To insure Smith's defeat at the polls, the Klan whipped up a frenzied smear campaign targeting Smith's religion. One piece of campaign literature reproduced a photograph of Governor Smith at ceremonies opening a new tunnel from New York to New Jersey. However, the photograph's caption insisted he was actually standing in front of an Atlantic tunnel connected to Rome that he secretly built to bring the Pope to America.

In the election, Smith only carried half of the South, Massachusetts, and Rhode Island, and lost all other states. The Klan may have cost him states in the "Solid South"—but these probably would have voted against a Catholic without Klan prodding. (Humorists joked that Smith sent a one-word telegram to the Vatican: "Unpack.")

It was a time of world peace and nationally it was an era of Republican popularity and prosperity. No Democrat could have overcome that combination. Smith was defeated by Republicanism and Herbert Hoover, not by The Invisible Empire's bigoted campaign. In losing, Smith still made significant inroads for his party among ethnic minorities and laboring people in cities of the North and West. Franklin D. Roosevelt would greatly expand on this new base during four successful campaign walks to the White House.

The KKK claim it had defeated Smith was part of a last-ditch effort to stave off collapse. Candidates no longer wanted open Klan backing, and The Invisible Empire had to back sure winners so they could claim victories. To avoid defeat for their favorites, the hooded order dared not openly aid them. Sometimes the Klan had to denounce candidates that they favored to insure their election. In Oregon, which they once ruled, they supported a candidate they hated—to defeat him!

Once it had been a respected and feared, rollicking Invisible Empire, but now it was reeling downhill. Upper and middle class people originally besieged Klan officials for membership applications. Now these prominent citizens began to hide their hoods and gowns in the attic, and seek more peaceful recreation. Admired community figures decided it would be better for their careers if they publicly apologized.

Slowly the medley of antagonisms and contradictions tearing at the hooded order unraveled in public. The Klan claimed to represent Christian charity yet it called for blood. Its members tried to isolate themselves from a sinful world and yet their battle plan included charging into other people's private lives. It preached brotherhood, yet it tore families apart, pitted husband against wife, parents against children, neighbor against neighbor.

Klan members were not brave but bewildered Protestants searching vainly for life's meaning; their leaders were not models of morality but petty con-men scooping out Klan treasuries. Its stated mission was to uphold law and order, yet the Klan constantly took the law into its own soiled hands. It caused disorder by acting as a rowdy, selfish policeman and censor.

Klan crusaders warned about sinister overseas plots directed from the Vatican or the Kremlin, but its whips cut the backs of innocent Americans. Its propaganda barrages aimed at dangerous aliens and Catholics, yet most of its victims were White, Protestant men and women. Its targets were not Catholic prelates or Soviet agents but ordinary citizens who looked very much like the people hiding under the sheets and hoods.

12

CORRUPTION
AND DECLINE

SOMETIME AROUND 1925, THE INVISIBLE EMPIRE, abandoned by the rich and middle classes, lost its spruced-up, buttoned-down look. When Klan parades shuffled through cities and towns in the United Staes, hoods and robes hid identities. But now there was a difference in the marchers' shoes. Once many wore expensive, well-polished models. That had changed. An eyewitness reported "a broken ripple of old shoes, square-toed, cracked, run over at the heels."

In 1926, Grand Wizard Hiram Evans wrote "We are a movement of the plain people, very weak in the matter of culture, intellectual support, and trained leadership. . . .This is undoubtedly a weakness. It lays us open to the charge of being 'hicks' and 'rubes' and 'drivers of second-hand Fords.' We admit it." Evans liked to call himself "the most average man in America." He now presided over citizens distinguished only by their undying hatred of certain fellow Americans and some foreigners they had heard rumors about.

The Ku Klux Klan of the Twenties attracted millions and proclaimed itself a huge success. Its pronouncements thundered in the land and politicians heeded. Klan policies won public acceptance, Klan votes elected hundreds to high office and Klan prejudices were enshrined in state and Federal laws.

The Invisible Empire's victories for bigotry were many. Congress severely restricted immigration to the United States by non-Protestants. Catholics, Jews, Germans, Russians, and other "foreigners" were viewed with great suspicion. Klan intimidation of Italian and French people in America reached a crescendo so upsetting that counsels for France and Italy formally protested to the US government.

Intolerance at home and isolationism abroad had captivated the hearts of citizens and the votes of Congressmen. Blacks clamoring for equal rights were beaten back North and South. Trade unions lost public respect and half of their membership. The tiny US Communist party became a pariah and barely avoided being crushed by Federal authority.

But even with a membership in the millions, was it the Klan that fused these moods and carried these policies to success? The Invisible Empire was only the noisiest trumpeter of isolationism, union-busting, and intolerance. In the ranks of haters, the Klan was bringing up the rear, not setting policy.

The Klan had to share victories with many other bigoted organizations, individuals, and politicians who had launched campaigns before Klansmen lit the first cross. And long after giant Klaverns slipped from the political scene, isolationism and racial and religious bigotry flourished in America.

The Ku Klux Klan did not keep the Pope in Rome from capturing the United States, for that was not his interest. It did not prevent a Communist revolution because none threatened. It did not halt a Jewish conspiracy from seizing the country, because no plot existed. The words and deeds spewing from the Klan volcano did not further Christian or democratic values.

The Klan did not keep young people from dancing to jazz music, petting in parked cars, or disobeying their parents. It did not drive up church attendance or slow down the divorce rate. The Invisible Empire did not defeat immorality, but increased it through its own roaring corruption and violence.

Klan rumors of terrifying conspiracies made untold numbers terribly uncomfortable or emotionally upset. It ripped through the lives of decent citizens who were Black, Jewish, Catholic, foreign-born, union members, drinkers, feminists, atheists, noncomformists, radicals, liberals, fun-seekers—or Protestants like themselves. For too many, the Klan cyclone brought death, maiming, or humiliation.

Its campaigns led to dismissals of Catholic, Jewish, and Black teachers and professionals. Its boycotts pierced minority businesses and derailed some promising careers. It discouraged young members of minorities from climbing ladders of success.

Klan abuse summoned forth a patchwork-quilt resistance. People of different religions, views and races who had never worked together

A lynching in March, 1928. (Library of Congress)

before united against the storm. They bravely challenged hooded figures who insisted only White Protestant men counted. In 1929, Robert Bagnall, a Black reporter, uncovered a South where some "white men both speak and act" against racism. Writing at the end of a Klan decade, he said:

> I know southern whites who have given up father, mother, home, and hopes of inheritance, in order to cling to their beliefs, that men and women are to be made comrades on the basis of congeniality regardless of color. "My father died in my arms without forgiving me," said one of these to me, "because of my position on race matters, but I am happy, for I have found something worthwhile in life."

The Ku Klux Klan first began to skid downhill when its hooded and armed marchers brawled in the streets of Middle America. They sang "Onward Christian Soldiers," but they could not hide the fact they came to battle fellow Christians, not godless foreign armies. The Klan began to lose its vaunted claim to moral superiority, and many gained a reputation for cowardice.

During these harrowing outbreaks, sheriffs and police cracked down on Klan violence. They impartially disarmed or arrested those who disturbed the peace. Even in the South where traditional White supremacy gave Klansmen a cloak of legitimacy, the Klan could not scorch or tear at fellow Whites without colliding with lawmen.

If the local police and sheriffs nationwide showed any leaning, it was probably toward their home town folks—fathers, uncles, brothers, and sons—who stood up to the torrent of intruders. Few authorities shrugged off Klan crimes or permitted hooded criminals to escape the impartial arrest net. This failure deprived it of a leading propaganda forum. Without street bullying, it could not stampede citizens to its ranks.

The Klan was dragged down further by its own insatiable thirst for other people's money. Eager recruiters signed up anyone with a ten dollar bill. One scholar undertook research to discover if the Klan had ever turned down any Protestant adult male who applied for membership. His answer was no.

Corruption and theft plagued the street order from its earliest Klaverns. In 1916, Imperial Wizard Simmons found a "traitor in the ranks" who had stolen "all of our accumulated funds." For the next decade and a half, Klan treasurers packed suitcases full of members' money and skipped town.

Officers could not account for funds collected, even huge amounts. And it was unsafe to ask. One New York Grand Kleagle, when asked about the Ulster County's funds, stroked his revolver, talked of violence and looked dead ahead.

In many localities, the biggest news was the armed rivalry that engulfed Klaverns. Factions hired spies to watch other factions. For dominance over a regional headquarters, a local treasury or high posts, Klansmen loaded guns and opened fire.

Here was a "high classs order" spreading "Christian virtue"—and being systematically looted by local directors. Followers, urged to donate their dollars and time in the battle against world evil, saw their heroes make off with the crusade's money.

Klansmen who raced into city politics promising reform profited heavily from vice. In Indiana, Klan officials did not drive out bootleggers, but licensed them. In Denver, the KKK police chief ruled an empire of gambling, liquor, and prostitution. Publicly The Invisible Empire supported Prohibition, but privately leaders drank as much as others, and bent their political influence to provide beer and liquor for their friends.

But these were minor embarrassments compared to what was happening at national headquarters in Atlanta. Millions of ten, five, and one dollar bills poured in and became an irresistible pond in which leaders fished with greedy fingers. When members asked for a financial accounting there was no response.

Between 1920 and 1925, more than $40,000,000 was collected and no one knows exactly what happened to it. Leaders routinely padded payrolls and used charity funds to fatten their bank accounts, buy fancy homes, planes and new cars.

In 1922, Simmons was maneuvered out of Klan control by his trusted associates. Told that his renomination would detonate armed warfare at a convention, he retired. They persuaded him to pick Hiram Evans, a Texas dentist , as Imperial Wizard.

When Simmons discovered the treachery, he plotted a full-scale counter-attack. He sent two secret agents into the Atlanta headquarters to steal $170,000 in cash and key documents. With these documents and his proof of copyright of the Klan name, ritual and costumes, he brought suit against Evans in court, and won.

As huge amounts of money piled higher in Atlanta, he sued Evans a second time for squandering funds. The two noisily settled matters in

Grand Wizard Hiram Evans, Washington, DC, 1926. (Library of Congress)

court. Simmons received $146,000 and Evans gained the reins of the secret order. But before it was over a Simmons' man had run off with $50,000 and an Evans' man had assassinated a Simmons' lawyer. The killer narrowly escaped execution—by claiming he was a "dangerous paranoid."

Each personal and financial revelation in court made large newspaper headlines and juicy stories. What Klan officials said about one another's fitness and character proved more damaging than charges hurled by enemies. In the full glare of publicity, a Christian crusade was furiously scratching and kicking over money. Endlessly, Klan missionaries wrangled privately and publicly and over dimes and dollars.

Hitler and his Nazi followers use racial prejudice to gain power and support in Europe. (Library of Congress)

During the Klan heyday, similar terrorist movements expanded in Europe. Hitler's brownshirts and Mussolini's blackshirts arrogantly stepped out to smash unions, communists, and Jews, and impose military and racist dictatorships. In Germany, it was called Nazism and in Italy it was Fascism, but it looked and sounded like the KKK of Indiana, Texas, or Oklahoma. While European fascists seized the reins of government, Klansmen slipped and slid downhill. There were reasons.

In Italy and Germany in the 1920s, fascist street gangs brought their nasty war into the streets of weak governments. Laughing stormtroopers roamed through towns cracking heads, wrecking meetings, and terrorizing their rivals. When the Nazi's foes were bloodied in the gutter, German lawmen did not appear.

Nazis stomped on enemies, but it was democracy that was ground underfoot. A German republic surrendered because its leaders believed radicals were far more dangerous than Nazi terror. Authorities cracked down on socialists, communists, and liberals. But local policemen, magistrates, and a legal system shrugged passively when Nazis brutally smashed the opposition.

This also served as guerrilla theater that changed political thinking— some citizens began to view Nazi terror in a new light. "At least the Nazis are doing something," became one response to a drowsy, ineffective state. Voters seriously discussed a new way to end the bloodshed: place Hitler and his armed forces in charge. "Power will make Hitler a responsible leader," said gullible people. Nazi street rioting had not only destroyed respect for democracy, but managed to win over some voters who hated disorder and fascism.

US Klansmen lost the battle of the streets, and so lost the fight for people's minds. Klansmen in the United States found they could not break necks or kick enemies into the gutter and strut arrogantly away. Lawmen consistently disarmed and led them—and other lawbreakers—to jail. Like European fascists, The Invisible Empire needed a passive or cooperative police and court system. Only rarely or briefly did it receive such cooperation.

In popularity, however, the Klan in the United States leaped ahead of the fascists in Germany or Italy. In the early 1920s, it received better publicity, as well as widespread admiration as Christian shock troops. Their candidates rolled up more votes than did their counterparts in Europe. This momentum however never climbed into permanent gains.

Unlike Europe's fascists, The Invisible Empire never rose to power. It hardly tried. Klansmen were half-hearted amateurs with a different quest. Members happily plunged into the privacy of fellow citizens while leaders dipped into wallets.

Fascism postponed greed in favor of a distant goal. Hitler and Mussolini learned that only an organization that masters its internal parts can seize power. Greed and individual corruption in the ranks must be banished or managed. Hitler personally established a special Nazi court that settled divisive disputes over leadership or cash. To prepare for something bigger, the European fascists disciplined their troops.

In 1922, Mussolini had his brownshirts march on Rome, and a panicky King Victor Emmanuel handed Mussolini the government. The next year, from a Munich beer hall, Hitler's stormtroopers sallied forth to

Hitler marched Jews, Gypsies, Easter Europeans and other "inferiors" into death camps.

seize control of Germany, and failed. A decade later, Hitler became Chancellor of Germany. By this time, Mussolini—now Il Duce—had slain or jailed his foes, established a dictatorship, and prepared for foreign adventures.

In Rome and Berlin, a Klan-like program was placed on track. In Europe, two dictators hurried bigotry toward a fearful genocide, and soon swaggered toward world domination.

The Invisible Empire had a different hunger. Local Kleagles constantly scrapped over cash and fought one another for leadership. Imperial Wizards never curbed local Kleagles' lust for money, liquor or women. In Indiana, dynamic Klansman David Stephenson was clapped in jail not for plotting treason but for kidnapping and manslaughter. By contrast, Hitler went to prison for an armed attempt to seize power in Munich, Germany.

With their soaring popularity, The Invisible Empire could have reached higher into government than it did. It was warmly and openly welcomed in the Democratic party in the South and in the Republican party nationwide. Its influence on Congressmen, Senators, and Judges skyrocketed to somewhere between impressive and staggering.

The Klan failed to stretch its political muscles to their natural limits. Its leadership failed to make The Invisible Empire decisive within either party. The Klan hierarchy never shaped its ideology into a cohesive, alluring political creed.

Perhaps these tasks represented too much hard work or too much deep thought. Perhaps these steps required a vision it lacked. The Klan never produced a dedicated demagogue with the magnetic force of a Hitler. Perhaps it did not want one.

Klan leaders signed on for personal gain, not the construction of a modern totalitarian state. Ranting against communist, Catholic, or Jewish plots was sufficient, and these urgent perils did not require Klan rule. Pointing them out was enough.

The Invisible Empire did not ride to power as did fascists in Europe because US life was calm and Europe's highly explosive. Post-war, devastated Italy and Germany were mired in huge unemployment and runaway inflation, and were rocked with workers' uprisings. Famine and economic turmoil led to unending riots. Anguished, jobless men numbered in the millions and considered desperate, revolutionary schemes. Citizens seriously wondered if fire, knife, and cannon might lead to national salvation.

Wealthy and middle-class Europeans became irrational. Terrified of losing their property and comfortable positions in a "Red Revolution," they eventually cast their lot with fascists. To keep workers or "Reds" from a hand in government, they would have financed the Devil. Frightened out of their conservatism, bankers and industrialists wrote checks to the fascist campaign chest. Their sons became fascist officers.

In the United States, the Twenties was not a decade when the wealthy people dreamed of a totalitarian dictatorship. They were piling up, not losing money or property. Their thugs had chopped down trade union and radical resistance. Workers looked no further than trying to keep their jobs and families fed. Revolutionaries were loud, but few and ineffective. Most whites enjoyed a relatively high standard of living, and looked forward not to starvation but bigger homes and better gadgets.

With Harding, Coolidge, and Hoover in the White House, the upper and middle classes could afford to relax. Capitalists counted huge profits and were pleased with Washington.

The Invisible Empire heard no higher calling. It was presided over by men whose selfish appetites spun merrily out of control. Fast-talking, small-minded hucksters, they galloped after immediate gain. They made news fighting one another for the Klan's bountiful harvest of cash. Hitler and Mussolini directed corrupt and craving men, but enforced an iron restraint. It is hard to believe that in the Twenties an Invisible Empire Administration could have sat in Washington, DC

The Modern
Invisible Empire:
1929 to Today

13

A REVIVED KLAN
MEETS RESISTANCE

BY 1929, THE HUGE KLAN KLAVERNS of the South had shrunk in size, and many in the North had faded from view. Only an estimated 100,000 die-hards remained active. But the stock market crash and the Great Depression could present a gold mine of opportunities, so Klansmen waited.

The Klan retreated below the Mason-Dixon line, and again focused on Black targets. Jews, "Reds," foreigners, and union organizers were still tied to a "world communist conspiracy." But anti-Catholic rhetoric became less prominent, and interference in private matters required too much manpower. Besides, it infuriated Whites and brought out local lawmen.

The Klan cross regularly burst into flames when Black families almost anywhere in the United States moved into "White neighborhoods." Klansmen regularly rode through southern Black ghettoes on election day as a warning to would-be voters.

But the 1930s were not the 1920s. There were no massive boycotts of Jewish, Black or Catholic store-owners and professionals. Gone were the huge night rallies that drew thousands of thrilled men, women and children. Membership drives failed to bring in newcomers. Senator Heflin's blatant anti-Catholic lectures lost him his Senate seat in Alabama, and he was swamped in two attempts to regain it.

During the Great Depression, a terrifying Ku Klux Klan became transformed into a largely social organization. It brought men and women together for beer and fun at picnics, not mayhem and murder. Politicians in the South rarely claimed Klan support, and northerners almost never. With joblessness mounting, dollars scarce, and men busy looking for work, the Klan slipped further.

One reason for this flagging interest in The Invisible Empire was a new sense of neighborliness, friendship and tolerance that vaulted over

Preparing to join a parade, 1920s.

traditional boundaries. The economic hard times did not stimulate racial division, but a new cooperative spirit. "We're in the same boat, brother," went a popular tune of the day. Despite unemployment of a third of the work force, competition for jobs did not drive Whites into the Klan.

Radical parties, such as socialists and communists, made headway and demanded equality and Black voting rights. In 1931, Communists began the defense of nine Black youths framed in Alabama for rape. Their world-wide protest saved the nine from execution, and more conservative forces took over their defense and eventually won their release. Radicals made public issues of Klan brutality, racial inequality and lynchings in the South. People began to listen.

In 1932, James Ford, a Black man, was nominated for Vice President on the Communist ticket. That same year a young Black communist organizer, Angelo Herndon, who defied the Klan to lead Black and White demonstrators, organized an integrated unemployment march through the streets of Atlanta. Arrested for insurrection, and causing "a combination of . . . White and colored," he faced execution—under a statute outlawing slave revolts. He was rescued from death or the chain gang by Benjamin Davis, a Black Atlanta attorney, who later was twice elected to the New York City Council.

During the hard times, more than radicals leaped forbidden racial boundaries. There were integrated bread lines and soup kitchens, and Black and White hunger marchers shared food and swapped stories. In 1932, when the Bonus Expeditionary Force of 15,000 unemployed veterans converged on the Capital, a reporter found "blacks were shot all through the B.E.F." "Things is different here than down home," said a Black North Carolinian.

In Greenville, South Carolina, William Anderson, 19, and a school janitor, led a Black voter registration drive. The young Black stood up to Klansmen, and waved his finger in a Kleagle's face. He was arrested 11 days later, charged with phoning a White female student, and spent 30 days in jail. But the drive for rights was not to be turned around by lawmen or Klansmen.

In Arkansas, sharecroppers who formed a union had to fight their bosses and attacks from local lawmen. An organizer was startled to find his members included Klansmen and Black sharecroppers—who together worked out strike strategies.

The huge hunger marches, demonstrations and strikes that united Black and White poor against the ravages of joblessness and starvation, set the Klan back. The secret order called these protests "communist inspired," but often feared to challenge them. In communities filled with starving and jobless people, it was harder, not easier to recruit lynchers.

The Invisible Empire had to tread carefully, and that proved a tall order. Klansmen soon joined the loudest voices shouting that President Franklin Roosevelt was a socialist, his name was really "Rosenfelt" and his New Deal was really a "Jew Deal."

Shocking for the Klan was that some of its worst enemies were standing tall. During the hard times, radicals and unions, taking leadership in campaigns to raise living standards, soared in public esteem. American citizens developed a tolerant attitude toward Soviet communism since it proved immune to the world's economic collapse and massive unemployment.

President Roosevelt's expanding Federal government hired Catholics and Jews in key posts, placed a woman, Frances Perkins, in the Cabinet, as well as meeting with an advisory "Black Cabinet," led by educator Mary McLeod Bethune. The President shocked fellow Protestants by reminding them "that all of us, and you and I especially, were descended from immigrants and revolutionists." This daring challenge from the White House made some furious, but it made others rethink their views. It did not please the Klan or build its membership.

Depression period of the 1930s. Vegetable pickers in Florida waiting to be paid. (Library of Congress)

In the Summer of 1934, Imperial Wizard Hiram Evans announced his organization stood against the "communism of FDR and the Jews" in the White House, and for what he called "constitutionalism." Klansmen again claimed they sought a return to an older, orderly America. Wealthy businessmen talked of replacing the President with a dictator of their choice, but the KKK was never a part of their plans. It had fallen from grace, even among people who shared its views.

In Florida, where the Klan was strongest, men announced "this is still a White man's country" and rode out to keep Black people from voting. Night riders also concentrated on terrorizing "unfaithful" married people, and couples in parked cars.

The Invisible Empire waged a full-scale war against the new industrial

Eleanor Roosevelt (center) in the audience as Pete Seeger entertains at an USO canteen in Washington, DC. 1944. (Library of Congress)

unions of the Congress of Industrial Organizations (CIO). They hunted down, tortured and sometimes murdered union organizers, especially if locals were biracial. For these assaults, they received important aid from southern mill owners, and public recognition. Anti-unionism in the 1930s involved major Klan resources and manpower.

The Invisible Empire worked hard at aligning its philosophy to causes it hoped would become popular. It joined with those who tried to keep FDR from being reelected to the Presidency—and failed three times. The Invisible Empire joined foes of the New Deal who were particularly infuriated by Eleanor Roosevelt. The President's high-spirited wife championed the causes of minorities, immigrants, and unions. She served as a sponsor of the first anti-lynching art show. In a further break from White House tradition, she was photographed with Black people. Massive propaganda assaults against Eleanor never discouraged her from spreading her views or helping minorities.

Though the Klan refused to fade, neither did it flower with the hard times as its leaders had predicted. Northern politicians avoided appeals for Klan support; even in the South, except for Georgia and Florida, it

The new unions became a leading target of the KKK.

was easier to win an election by laughing at The Invisible Empire than by endorsing it.

The New Deal of FDR, the daring of Eleanor, the work of radicals, and particularly the militancy of minorities had initiated a new era in US racial relations. A growth of tolerance began that no Invisible Empire could turn around.

In 1939, a frustrated KKK in Greenville, South Carolina, could only warn Blacks not to "continue to register and vote." In Miami, Florida, Klansmen burned 25 crosses, armed and marched through Miami's Black voting precincts. But Sam Solomon, a Black businessman, asked the 1,500 registered blacks to walk with him to the polls and on election day 1,000 bravely joined him.

* * * * *

The rise of fascist power in Europe had been warmly welcomed by US Klansmen. They not only admired Hitler and Mussolini, but treated their racial arrogance and discrimination codes as useful models. They distributed Nazi pamphlets.

In 1940, the Ku Klux Klan finally held a joint meeting with the pro-Nazi "German-American Bund" at Nordland, New Jersey. Speakers from each side praised one another's efforts for "the master race," and enthusiastically recalled battles waged against communists, Jews, blacks, unions, and foreigners. The swastika and the burning cross were united on New Jersey soil.

In less than two years, US soldiers marched off to destroy a mighty Nazi war machine and the master race who directed its bid for world domination. The Ku Klux Klan support dried up, and the Imperial Wizard rushed off to Washington in a desperate effort to unite Jews and Catholics behind his patriotism. During the struggle against Nazi fascism, the Klan took a vacation.

In May, 1945, Hiram Evans, who led The Invisible Empire during its Twenties popularity, died. His death came just as Allied armies began liberating the Nazi concentration camps.

A shocked world began to learn how Nazi racial policies had led to the genocide of eight million people. Through flickering newsreels, the Third Reich's massacre of "racially inferior" men, women and children was seared into memories. It was clear where Klanism, administered by one nation, could lead.

But The Invisible Empire was merely wounded and far from dead. In 1946, from atop Stone Mountain, Georgia, where William Simmons had led his little band in 1915, a renewed Invisible Empire was launched. "We are revived!" yelled new members.

A membership drive lagged—perhaps it was too soon after the Nazi "holocaust" to attract many to The Invisible Empire. People who now wore Klan hoods and gowns were categorized somewhere between dangerous, dumb, or silly.

The postwar world, however, was filled with the kind of painful dislocations that Klansmen might exploit. Minorities demanded their fair share of the American Dream and boldly stepped into the US mainstream. Black ex-soldiers were determined to win some of the democracy they had helped save in World War II. Women wanted to keep the decent jobs they had captured during the war.

Minorities and foreigners were fast becoming major city populations. Protestants continued to diminish in numbers and influence, and the "old time religion" was slipping again. The ease at which people moved around the country or into jobs led to greater family stress. A rural America had shrunk to a fraction of its former size and an alluring way of life called suburbia mushroomed everywhere. People greeted these changes with a mixture of anxiety, fear, and excitement.

On the international scene, nuclear war hung over the world. Since the Soviet Union had been decisive in defeating world fascism and its armed might now sat in Europe, communism loomed larger than before. Third World colonies fought their way from colonialism to freedom. This unheard part of the world spoke eloquently from the United Nations building.

Most citizens viewed members of The Invisible Empire as part of an age that had passed away, a dinosaur best ignored. Radio and newspaper reporters ridiculed and exposed Klan antics and slogans. A White writer, Stetson Kennedy, infiltrated the KKK and revealed its secrets in *Southern Exposure.*

The FBI finally began tracking the most violent Klansmen, and Attorney General Tom Clark placed the organization on his subversive's list, along with the U.S. Communist party. More Pulitzer Prizes in journalism were awarded for Klan exposures, than for any other single topic. On radio, Walter Winchell and Drew Pearson flayed the KKK, and even Superman's audience heard him trounce the cowardly bigots.

Klan activities increasingly encountered local resistance. Public Klan cross-burnings more frequently drew White, Black, Catholic, Protestant, and Jewish hecklers and gigglers. Presidential candidate Henry Wallace cracked southern segregation and defied Klan threats by addressing mixed assemblies. Florida Governor Fuller Warren, a former member, denounced Klansmen as "hooded hoodlums. . .sheeted jerks. . .covered cowards."

Georgia, the southern Klan center, joined many cities that passed anti-mask laws. It became easier for southern courts to convict Klan lawbreakers—if their victims were White. Governors and Mayors publicly scorched The Invisible Empire.

By the 1950s, a daring new opposition to the hooded order was started by its principal victims. In 1957, Monroe, North Carolina Blacks and Native Americans defied the Invisible Empire. Both groups had the satisfaction of seeing Klansmen turn and run.

Black efforts in Monroe to desegregate swimming pools for children brought the hooded order into the open. Nightly, Klan motorcades rumbled through the black community, honking horns and shotgun blasting at windows.

The Monroe NAACP, under Robert Williams, protested to the city council, and nothing happened. He asked for protection from state and Federal government officials and again received no aid or encouragement. Finally, under Williams, the Black community "started arming ourselves." This time when the Klan sent an armed motrocade, Williams reported:

> We shot it out with the Klan and repelled their attack and the Klan didn't have any more stomach for this type of fight. They stopped raiding our community. After this clash the same city officials who said the Klan had a constitutional right to organize met in emergency session and passed a city ordinance banning the Klan from Monroe without a special permit from the police chief.

Two weeks later, Klansmen tried to disturb the peaceful Lumbee Indians, a mixture of Red, Black and White races. They had no intention of permitting sworn enemies to burn a cross and hold a meeting on their doorstep. As Klansmen prepared to light a huge cross, 500 armed Lumbees charged, firing guns and yelling.

The armed night riders took off, abandoning their speaker system to the laughing Lumbees. The State Police arrived in time to restore order and send the Lumbees home. The only injuries sustained were to the Klan's speaker system.

By the beginning of the 1950s, the United States, as "leader of the free world," increasingly came under scrutiny and criticism for it's failure to protect Black lives. In 1951, the noted actor and baritone Paul Robeson and civil rights advocate William L. Patterson delivered a petition to the United Nations entitled "We Charge Genocide." It dealt with deaths inflicted on Black Americans by lynching, legal execution and police brutality.

Led by NAACP attorneys, Black people successfully pursued anti-discrimination cases in court. They gained rights to attend schools and colleges, fairer employment practices and greater access to public facilities and housing.

Even in the segregated southland, this progress provoked a growing White understanding that Klan actions aggravated racial problems. With the Klan receiving less public support and less protection from local governments, the number of lynchings dropped sharply.

14

AT WAR WITH THE
CIVIL RIGHTS MOVEMENT

ON MAY 17, 1954, U.S. RACE relations changed forever and with it the sagging fortunes of the Ku Klux Klan. US Supreme Court justices unanimously affirmed the legal arguments of NAACP attorneys and found school segregation—after 88 years—in violation of the US Constitution. They ordered its end "with all deliberate speed."

Segregationists responded with a hysterical call for total resistance. The Klan proclaimed "the defense of southern white womanhood" and announced blood would run in school corridors. The stage was set for a revival of The Invisible Empire, and new members reached for their whips and guns.

Klan propaganda zeroed in on an emerging figure in the fight for equal rights. Dr. Martin Luther King, Jr. first stepped into leadership during the 1955 Montgomery Bus boycott. After more than a year of agitation, his followers' disciplined use of nonviolent resistance led to victory. Awed by his effectiveness, segregationists called him "Martin Lucifer King."

To meet the needs of fearful Whites, The Invisible Empire expanded its operations. By 1958, Georgia membership rose to close to 15,000, and there were seven competing secret orders.

J.B. Stoner, active as a Klansman since 18, leaped into the fray with plans to do away with Blacks and Jews who, he stated, were taking over the United States. He headed the National States Rights Party and drew inspiration from Adolph Hitler and his Nazi stormtroopers. For this Klan organization, Stoner borrowed the SS symbol of the Nazi elite troops in charge of concentration camps and the genocidal death of "inferiors."

Most White people stood by while extremists took charge. Representing this community sentiment, local officials overtly or covertly opposed the Black drive for equality—and failed to protect Black families from Klan-type lawlessness.

A woman in Dallas, Texas, in 1956, points to a segregation sign that will be removed the next day. (United Press International)

A Reconstruction era cast of characters again made their appearance in the South. Klansmen, served as the cutting edge for segregationists, and slashed at Blacks or Whites who accepted the new law of the land. Soon White and Black northern college students came to assist southern Blacks gain voting rights and an education. Some local Whites, believing this struggle was in the best tradition of resistance to tyranny also aided Black neighbors.

White Citizens Councils, a new racist organization, formed all over the South to crush Black people through economic and legal pressures. They were destined to play a more crucial role than the Klan in combatting the Civil Rights crusade. Much as prominent citizens of the first Klan era provided the hooded riders with secret legal and political strength, these councils sought to halt integration by similar but more effective means.

The Federal government, as it had for a century, declared that desegregation would be handled at local levels, without its intervention. It proposed to let matters slide. President Eisenhower never publicly supported the Supreme Court decision, and privately said he disagreed with it. Klan violence, as usual, was considered a local or state police matter. No Federal troops were dispatched to southern school districts.

After some school districts in the upper South and the North desegregated, matters rested silently on legal paper. But racial relations in the United Staes have never long remained both lopsided and quiet. Neither Klansmen nor Black citizens were willing to accept a stalemate. As southern schools and universities began the process of integrating token Blacks into their student bodies, Klan violence flared.

But this time thousands of young men did not reach for guns and flock to the ranks of The Invisible Empire. The Southern White majority had shifted. Fewer White people believed in the value of intimidation and death, and even fewer volunteered to carry them forth. Black people were ready to move faster than ever before, and even terrorism could not hold them down.

Another sign of changing times was the election of John F. Kennedy, a Catholic, to the Presidency with only a snarl from religious bigots. Al Smith's notion that a Catholic could win the US Presidency finally was vindicated.

New aspects of racism had surfaced in the years following World War II. As "leader of the free world," and vulnerable to criticism, the US had to intervene to halt racial turmoil. To enforce a Federal court order that protected 9 Black students in Little Rock, Arkansas, President Eisenhower dispatched 1,000 troops of the 101st Airborne. The belated process of Federal intervention slowly was being deployed.

Southern businessmen saw their sales and investments sent plummeting by constant Klan attacks, Black defiance and racial turbulence. They came to understand that their best interest would be served by promoting peaceful desegregation, and curbing the Klan. The advent of TV news coverage thrust bombings, murders and riots into millions of living rooms each night. Voters, disgusted with the absence of state law and order, demanded greater Federal intervention. The White South became a national disgrace, and the Ku Klux Klan its bloodsoaked symbol.

Segregationist banners were carried most effectively not by the insolent, violent Klansmen. The key counter-attack on integration was

Black student Elizabeth Eckford is driven away from White Central High School in Little Rock, Arkansas, in 1956. To enforce a court ordered desegregation in the school, President Eisenhower ordered in the 101st Airborne and Ms. Eckford was permitted to continue her education. (United Press International)

carried forth by charming, talkative, educated congressmen, Governors, Senators, and business leaders of the White Citizens Councils.

Because The Invisible Empire's violence did, at times, play a role that segregationists wanted, the hooded order was never outlawed. It had made inroads into law-enforcement, enrolling sheriffs, deputies and local judges. These lawmen stood ready to staunch the tide of resolute, marching Black southerners.

The Invisible Empire was usually led by men who barely clung to a middle-class status. They might run a gas station or a small general store or serve as a deputy sheriff. Everywhere around them was change and talk of equality for people they always considered inferior. With the tenacity of a slaveholder, they fought to uphold the racism of their ancestors.

Klan members at this time were usually people who had little education and felt insecure in a changing, modern America. Additionally, many saw themselves in competition with striving Blacks. They had come from rural districts and did not feel accepted in larger cities where they had settled. The Invisible Empire became a means to express feelings of fury and frustration over insecure positions and a way to blame and lash out at scapegoats. Interestingly, most members did not come from areas experiencing Civil Rights convulsions, but were from nearby towns relatively unaffected.

The Invisible Empire talked about and carried out violence. In the first four years after the Supreme Court decision, there were 530 cases of overt racial violence and intimidation—including 6 murders, 29 shootings, 44 beatings, 5 stabbings and the bombings of 30 homes, 7 churches, 4 Synagogues and 4 schools. In the tense battle over desegregation, 17 southern towns were threatened with mob violence. The Klan was involved in most.

In the 1950s, the Ku Klux Klan had added a new weapon to its arsenal: dynamite. With bombs, The Invisible Empire no longer singled out one or two people, but without warning, it could strike at many with murderous effectiveness. In 1951, Florida state NAACP director Harry Moore and his wife were blown up in their bedroom. Between 1956 and 1963, more than 130 homes, places of worship and businesses had been destroyed or damaged by explosions.

Scene from one of the many "Freedom Schools" conducted as part of the Mississippi Summer Project of 1964.

To explain the determination behind the Civil Rights movement, The Invisible Empire revived a scapegoat from the 1920s. "The Jewish Conspiracy" helped nourish anxieties and explained how supposedly happy, uneducated, penniless Blacks became militantly demanding. Jewish citizens were among the first Whites to become prominent supporters of or participants in the Black drive for equality. Blacks could not be associated with money, education, or power, but Jews could. "Blacks are the arms and legs," and "Jews are the brains," stated a Klan poster.

To attract support in its war against the Black march toward freedom, The Invisible Empire also revived a favorite adversary—world communism. Communist agents, it said, lurked behind almost every Black leader and the Civil Rights movement was manipulated from Moscow. For paranoid Whites, who could not comprehend that their Black neighbors simply wanted equal rights, conspiratorial theories proved useful.

As the Summer of 1964 approached, the Student Nonviolent Coordinating Committee (SNCC) planned a massive educational and voter registration "Freedom Summer" drive in Mississippi. But just as hundreds of White and Black college students began to arrive in Mississippi, the KKK struck first. Three young Civil Rights workers, a Black Mississippian, and two New York Jewish students were arrested for a traffic violation. Released that evening, they rode into a careful Klan trap.

Their car was overtaken by Klan raiders commanded by a chief deputy sheriff. The three were slain, their bodies buried in a dam. Largely because Whites were among the victims, world TV coverage and public outrage greeted the slayings. Federal agents swept into Mississippi. In 1967, a KKK Imperial Wizard, the county's chief deputy sheriff, and five others were sentenced to prison for Civil Rights violations, two for a maximum of ten years.

Before the FBI located the bodies, the *Klan-Ledger's Special Neshoba County Fair Edition* offered its version of events in question and answer format.

Q. What is your explanation of why there have been so many National Police Agents involved in the case of the "missing civil rights workers"?

A. First, I must correct you on your terms. Schwerner, Chaney, and Goodman were not civil rights workers. They were Communist Revolutionaries, working to undermine and destroy Christian Civilization. The blatant and outlandish National Police activity surrounding their case merely points up the political overtones of the entire affair. . . .

Q. By "political overtones" do you mean that the case has a bearing on the forthcoming elections?

A. It is doubtful that the case itself will be made an issue in the election. However, the incumbent in the White House [Lyndon Johnson] is a communist sympathizer, as proven by his numerous acts of treason, and his sole chance of victory in the November election will depend upon his being able to hold his communist-liberal bloc together by continuing to support and protect all Domestic Communists.

The Klan newsletter asked if Communists might not have committed the triple murder themselves. Its answer was:

137

A. ...The Communists never hesitate to murder one of their own if it will benefit the party. Communism is pure, refined, scientific Cannibalism in action. A case in point is the murdered [President John F.] Kennedy. Certainly, no President could have been a more willing tool to the Communists than was the late and unlamented "Red Jack." He cooperated with them at every turn. Yet. . .he was callously given up for execution by those whom he had served so well. . . .

The Klan ended on its traditional note of patriotic pride:

Q. Do the White Knights of the KU KLUX KLAN advocate or engage in unlawful violence?
A. We are absolutely opposed to street riots and public demonstrations of all kinds. Our work is largely educational in nature. . . .All of our work is carried on in a dignified and reverent manner. . . .We are Americans in the White Knights of the KU KLUX KLAN of Mississippi.

Against such self-righteous falsehoods and evils, Black Americans carried on the long, painful struggle for citizenship rights. They withstood violent public officials such as "Bull" Conner in Birmingham, and Jim Clark in Selma; they endured high-powered water hoses, snarling police dogs, and the arrest of thousands of children; they suffered lynchings, bombings and torture. Through their courageous, nonviolent response, Black people began to win increasing support in the South and the nation. By spotlighting and isolating their enemies, they moved closer to victory.

In September, 1963, in frustration over their failures, the KKK detonated a bomb during a Sunday school class at the 16th Street Baptist church in Birmingham, Alabama. Four little Black children, who had just been singing "The Love That Forgives," died in the blast. This senseless act of murder accomplished nothing, and the Klan bomber was eventually imprisoned.

President Kennedy, who initially opposed the "March on Washington," greets the march leaders at the White House on August 28, 1963. (United Press International) Left to right, front row: Whitney Young, National Urban League; Dr. Martin Luther King, Jr., Southern Christian Leadership Conference; Rabbi Joachim Prinz, chairman of American Jewish Congress; A. Philip Randolph, March Director; President Kennedy; Walter Reuther, vice-president, AFL-CIO; and Roy Wilkins, NAACP.

But despite severe losses, The Invisible Empire lingered. It tried to rebuild a crumbling membership through bloody combat against the civil rights demonstrators. It failed, not because white southerners favored equal rights, but because most realized the Klan gave bigotry a bad name.

When The Invisible Empire or others surfaced to wield weapons of violence, TV cameras captured the scenes of devastation and interviewed the victims. Voters became impatient, and a Federal court system, Congress, and the President increasingly had to protect all citizens. "I'm afraid, but I'm not terrorized," said one Black woman in 1963. These words meant Black people in effect had disarmed the Klan.

High point of the protest movement was the 1963 March on Washington in which more than a quarter million people participated. This was the largest demonstration in American history to that point. Unprecedented in size, the 1963 March was also unprecedented in its bringing together people of diverse racial, religious, cultural, and economic backgrounds. It paved the way for the passage of the 1964 Civil Rights Act that granted equal protection by the law and access to public facilities which constitutional amendments had promised since the end of the Civil War.

The next year, after peaceful marchers were assaulted by armed Alabama state troopers, President Johnson signed another law that sent Federal registrars to insure Black voting rights in the South.

These laws were first won on the streets and roads of southern communities by Black people who would not be turned around. Intimidation and violence by local officials and Klansmen, once so pervasive, were dramatically reduced. Black voters went to the polls and elected their own representatives.

The Klan still enjoyed some hidden support and remained alive. Bigots who would never themselves hurl bombs into homes or houses of worship, maim or shoot innocent people—knew they could count on The Invisible Empire. During the first Reconstruction, Klan violence led to White supremacy's victory. This time its sporadic explosions symbolized its frustrated rage at defeat.

15

MARCHING INTO
THE 1980s

THE INVISIBLE EMPIRE ROARED INTO THE 1980s with its leaders predicting a Klan decade. A sharp increase in membership began in the late 1970s, and activities ranged from cross-burning to assassinations and an election campaign in California.

As if to highlight their entrance into the new decade, on November 3, 1979, Klansmen gunned down five anti-KKK radicals holding a "Death to the Klan" rally in Greensboro, North Carolina. Those charged with murder were acquitted.

The Seventies ended with soaring inflation, mounting unemployment, a weak Carter presidency, and renewed fears of world communism. The secret order sought to shape that combination of domestic and foreign woes into a successful recruiting drive.

At the beginning of the 1980s, The Invisible Empire was represented by four competing groups. They had nothing nice to say about one another and were more likely to feud that cooperate. But since they were armed and threatened victims with a violence they were fully prepared to inflict, they were neither ineffective nor powerless. All four believed in the politics of cowardly attack and racial blood-letting.

In the early 1980s, Klan members were mechanics, gas station attendants, and factory laborers—and policemen, prison guards, and teachers. They were southerners and northerners, men and women, young and old, rich, poor and middle-class. There were a few of the very rich, a sprinkling of criminals, and some jobless people.

Teen-agers made up about 15% of the membership, and active Klan recruiting took place in schoolyards. Half of Klan recruits were between the ages of 18 and 35 and by zeroing in on youths still attending school, the Klan intended to grow. Smiling recruiters appeared in front of school doors during lunch hour or when classes let out.

By the 1980s, The Invisible Empire had revolutionized its recruitment policies and drastically altered its hate list. Catholics, once a leading Klan scapegoat, were actively sought. Union members, long a target of the hooded order, were now handed membership blanks. Women, shunned until the 1920s, were invited to join, and the recruited wives and girlfriends of male members, made up a fourth of total membership. They increasingly played an active role.

Protestants still constituted the largest portion of the membership and Klan propaganda appealed to them as an embattled "minority in their own land." The Invisible Empire's hate list focused heavily on such reliable, fearful victims as Blacks, Jews, communists, and liberals. As always, The Invisible Empire stood prepared to ride out at night for a hate-filled America, and strike at those whom it considered not "American" enough—and too weak to fight back.

As it had in the 1920s, the new Klan operated North and South. It established military training centers in Alabama, Texas, North Carolina—and in Illinois, California, and Connecticut. In July, 1980, 400 Whites attended an Illinois Klan camp to receive instruction in the use of guns, chemical warfare, explosives and "street action." Trainers, led by a former U.S. Colonel, wore Army uniforms and taught volunteers various ways to kill.

By 1981, more than 10,000 citizens paid dues to one KKK or another, and another 100,000 considered themselves friends and supporters of the hooded order. Klaverns mushroomed in half of the fifty states, and in all branches of the Armed Forces.

The Klan had climbed aboard aircraft carriers, jet planes and Army trucks. Klansmen in uniforms assaulted Black fellow soldiers, sailors and marines, and the US high command had to deal with serious Armed Forces morale problems.

The modern Klan sought out racial trouble spots. Its recruiters attempted to undo the progress in educational desegregation by exploiting tensions in integrated public schools. Their propaganda pitted one race and religion against another. Klansmen handed out leaflets asking White students to combat "grinning black thugs" and "stand up and fight for White students and their interests." They made inroads among students who never learned Klan history.

Recruitment among the young became intense, with Klan Youth

Corps centers located in San Diego, San Bernadino, and Los Angeles, California; Denver, Colorado; Chicago and Peoria, Illinois; Jefferson, Indiana; Hillsborough County, Florida; Oklahoma City, Oklahoma; and Birmingham, Tuscaloosa, Tuscumbia, and Decatur, Alabama. Everywhere the message was the same: the White race faces a deadly peril and must fight back. The Klan portrayed its foes as powerful in number and financial backing, and aided by cowardly state or Federal officials.

Beginning in the early 1980s, Klan leaders put on a new, modern face. They no longer looked, spoke or behaved like bigoted hoodlums with a criminal record. Spokesmen dressed in pin-striped or dark-flannel suits, drove sport cars and private planes and talked with an educated air on TV and radio. To emphasize their Christian goals, ministers were asked to address Klan meetings.

This new image was designed to aid Klansmen in soliciting funds and support from people who resented the brash, insulting, old-time bigots. But when the TV lights went out and leaders returned to their members, they served up that racial venom that has always nourished the secret order. Leaders did not use the word "nigger" in public, only to the faithful.

The Invisible Empire added some new victims to its targeted list of "foreigners." In Texas, it struck at Vietnamese fishermen it said were competing with White Texans. Though these people fled communism in Asia, it called them "communists." It singled out recent nonwhite immigrants from Haiti, gay people, Puerto Ricans, Chicanos, feminists, and pro-abortion people. It blamed the Federal government in Washington for the gains minorities had won through civil rights demonstrations. It charged that liberals in government and out permitted communism and atheism to conquer the United States.

More than a few Americans began listening to the quiet voices of The Invisible Empire in their new suits. As usual, they heard those attractive, simple answers to the baffling problems and unrelenting pressures of the 1980s. With plant closings, job firings, high interest rates and inflation dropping middle-class people into poverty during the Carter and Reagan years, it was easy to conjure up scapegoats. As adults and children worried about nuclear war, pollution of the environment, and the

143

insecurities of job, school or old age, the Klan waved its ready list of foes, and heated up its rhetoric.

The secret order had also emerged from the wings with some ill-informed, tough, angry words about foreign policy—and "sticking up for America." In 1980, *The Klansman* offered its glittering answer to declining U.S. prestige: "The nation is gravely in need of a mighty force to halt the Washington insanity and return our country to its position of greatness in the world."

They joined the angry shouts that called for warfare against Shiites in Iran, rebels in El Salvador and the Sandinistas in Nicaragua. Militant talk, the Klan had long ago discovered, always attracts media attention, arouses interest from potential members and costs nothing.

On the home front, the Klan emphasized such urban problems as crime, drugs, and job insecurity. Its propaganda routinely blamed minorities who were the leading victims of these problems. As city life became increasingly stressful and uncertain, the Klan reached out to new recruits using frightening words and talking of evil conspiracies.

Rather than examine an economic system that creates too few jobs, The Invisible Empire asked for work and promotions for Whites, not Blacks. It wrapped this Klan version of fairness in super-patriotic language and "that old time religion." Although it directed its appeals most often to working people, Klan programs consciously divided one group of laborers from another—when only unity could improve working conditions.

The Klan, in rejecting new life styles and "our permissive society," appealed to those who feared the future and looked back nostalgically at times when people appeared conforming, obedient, and accepting. It revived anxieties many people had about gay people, feminism, pornography, and legal abortions.

Offering a fantasy version of this past could not restore stability or preserve "moral values." Even recreating this distorted, mythological past increased people's normal anguish and the strain they felt over progress.

In the early 1980s, The Invisible Empire continued its long tradition of cowardly violence. Klansmen bombed churches, synagogues, and meeting halls and shot at innocent urban and rural victims. They

The Invisible Empire meetings in the 1980s are attended by women and children. (Stern/Black Star)

attacked a Black Civil Rights march in Decatur, Alabama, and nine Klansmen were finally indicted.

In Tennessee, Klan rifle fire wounded five elderly Black women peacefully passing the time of day in their neighborhood. In Texas, Klansmen set fire to Vietnamese fishing boats, and sent armed patrols across the water to assault these recent Asian immigrants to the Galveston Bay area.

Elsewhere the KKK, protected by the First Amendment, marched in public carrying its insulting signs. On July 4, 1977, a Klan rally was held on the steps of the state house in Columbus, Ohio. When the Grand Dragon sprayed mace on protesting Black youths, more Black and White protesters mobilized for a counter-demonstration, charged Klansmen, ripped off their sheets, and broke up their rally.

Beginning in the late 1970s, this resistance to the secret order became more militant. In 1977, Buddy Cochran, a White worker, drove his car into a Klan rally in Plains, Georgia, and was sentenced to jail. Some 110 robed Klansmen marched through Tallahassee, Florida, that same year seeking recruits. Instead, they were confronted by 1,500 young Black and White people shouting "Down With the Klan." Only police intervention saved the hooded marchers.

In Greensboro, North Carolina, members of The Invisible Empire and of the American Nazi party teamed up to attack radicals who were holding a "Death to the Klan" rally in a Black ghetto. The Greensboro police followed the Klan to the rally site, yet disappeared when the Klan opened fire, killing five young men and wounding others.

In the murder trial, videotapes by four TV crews showed the Klansmen arming for the massacre, but the accused were freed. In a 1985 damage suit, families of the nine radicals killed or wounded were awarded $351,500 from the city because local police were negligent or cooperated with the Klan gunmen.

The Greensboro case demonstrates anew that The Invisible Empire has always needed friends within government to escape prosecution for its criminal acts—and that it often has found them. Where law enforcement is firm, the violence halts. In June, 1982, a US District Judge banned the Texas Klan from conducting military training. That responsibility, she ruled, belongs to the government, and war training in Texas stopped.

The new-style Klansmen occasionally demonstrated an ability to generate northern political support. In 1980, Klansman Tom Metzger won the Democratic nomination for Congress from California's huge 43rd district (largest in the country) that includes northern San Diego. He lost the election but rolled up a total of 35,107 votes. Metzger announced that his staggering vote proved the Klan is representative of White society.

What was The Invisible Empire like—as seen from the inside during this time? Jerry Thompson, a reporter for the Nashville *Tennessean*, infiltrated the Klan for a year. He wrote a book on his secret mission saying that The Invisible Empire enjoyed considerable middle-class support. One Saturday he and other Klan members held a fund-raising drive at a busy intersection outside Birmingham, Alabama, and in three hours raised $1,100 from drivers of Cadillacs and Lincolns. Concluded Thompson:

The Ku Klux Klan today holds a strange, disturbing attraction

146

for frustrated, fearful middle-income men and women—and a dangerous potential for violence and terror.

The Invisible Empire of the early 1980s boasted arsenals of automatic weapons, wielded rifles in public, and carried forth its banners in the service of a divided America. "These guns ain't for killing rabbits," said Klansman Bill Wilkinson, "they're to waste people. We're not going to start anything, but if anyone does, we're ready to defend ourselves." The record shows who it is that initiates the violence Wilkinson boasted about.

Though their propaganda had been aimed specifically at minorities and "communists," a host of other innocents have appeared in Klan gunsights. Its targets have often been ordinary citizens and an entire justice and legal system. Jerry Thompson's experience convinced him of this:

I never really considered the Klan a threat to me--after all, I'm not Black, I'm not Jewish. But I'm aware now, and firmly believe, that as long as the Klan presents a threat to anybody, we're all threatened--as long as a single human lives under the influence of fear and intimidation, we all live under that influence.

16

THE MESSAGE HIDDEN
UNDER THE HOODS

THE INVISIBLE EMPIRE FIRST STEPPED INTO the limelight as a last refuge and terrorist strike force for White southerners who would not accept the verdict of the Civil War. During its reincarnations, Klansmen have unfurled an array of banners in addition to its original White supremacy flag. In this century, the KKK has been recognizable by its boasts of super-patriotism and racial superiority, its use of violence and intimidation, and its loathing for Americans and foreigners who are different. The hooded order explains its wrong-headed policies and brutal crimes with a Christianity and patriotism based on disproven racial theories and a misinterpretation of history and the Bible.

A bent version of America's legacy is a vital part of Klan thinking. Mentally, The Invisible Empire lives in a past of its own concoction. It manufactures dubious events, peoples them with distorted historical figures and offers these twisted myths as answers for current questions. In religion, politics, culture, and social attitudes, it yearns for the return of a heritage that never was.

To meet today's difficult problems, the Klan offers the slogan "stand up for America," and with such catchy phrases as "forced busing," "reverse discrimination," and "world communism," it attacks foes and seeks to ensnare new recruits. As the United States, the most awesome nuclear power in the world, flounders like a helpless giant, Klan simplifications have some appeal.

The strength and impact of the secret order in this century stems from its ability to strike a resonant White chord in a multi-racial society. Though the Klan has consistently misread the past, it has hit upon a simple truth that does much to keep its engine fueled and running: White people do not want to surrender their privileges, and many do not wish to share any part of the American pie with "others." The erroneous notion that only Whites built this country is used as the basic argument to justify this claim to special privilege.

Many people, its victims first, wish that the Klan—like a dracula—would disappear with the first rays of morning. It would be comforting to conclude this last chapter with the judgment that the Klan's days are numbered, but this would be an inaccurate reading of its record and normal course.

The Invisible Empire, its slick leaders and language, and its crude violence will continue to swell at certain moments of national weakness. It once had monied families, major landowners, bankers and industrialists in its camp, but has not held this kind of support since the 1920s. Still, for some time to come, its ranks will be filled with and its bills paid by the generosity of the anxious and the kindness of the angry.

If there is a positive side to the presence of Klansmen among us, it is that they inform us of an unresolved, destructive fury lurking in the body politic. Klan crimes are a constant reminder that injuries, punished when committed against Whites, are rarely punished when nonwhites are the victims. The hooded order tells us how needed is an accurate version of our racial heritage and an impartial justice system.

The Invisible Empire has committed thousands of murders and many serious crimes during its six generations of life. but it did not invent nor bring racial or religious hatred to these shores. The Klan built on the fertile soil it found. Beginning with the arrival of Columbus, who enslaved and massacred Native Americans, seeds of racial violence were scattered and harvested by the most respected Whites.

Racism was affirmed in the Declaration of Independence, the US Constitution, and the highest laws of the land. After slavery ended, legal strategies and language were altered, but discrimination continued and national progress rested heavily on the exploitation of nonwhite labor. This and U.S. overseas expansion were justified by White supremacy doctrines.

Today, the Klan sticks out because it is the sorest thumb of an enduring American problem. If The Invisible Empire vanished, that would not mean that discrimination had faded away. The Klan will not disappear precisely because it often fits into America's racial duplicity and

The Ku Klux Klan burns a cross in Scotland, Connecticut in September, 1980.

acts as the cutting edge of a racial antagonism that has seeped into the bone marrow of White society. It retreats when it is confronted or exposed but when its enemies abandon the scene of battle, it strolls back.

Throughout history, political figures, from the President of the United States to Governors and local officials, have denounced Klan excesses. Sometimes these responses have been brave, even daring acts in defense of vulnerable citizens and institutions. At other times, such as the present, attacking The Invisible Empire can be rather like denouncing man-eating sharks: it wins hearty approval among voters. But it also changes nothing.

The Ku Klux Klan should not become a whipping boy or scapegoat for those who would rather avoid treating deeply embedded and less obvious examples of racism. Prosecuting Klan crimes is appropriate because society lives by the law. But actions against the Ku Klux Klan have no impact on racism and the problems it creates. Better schools, more jobs, improved neighborhoods, and greater security for minorities and all citizens, will derail any hate campaigns.

Today's minorities are denied their rights not by a small, screeching Invisible Empire, but by a legal and economic system that quietly accepts a view of US life based on White privilege. That is far harder to combat than gangs of insulting men carrying insolent signs and making bizarre threats.

When officials brand The Invisible Empire an atrocious, un-American organization, they are telling the truth. Their denunciations, however, can create a false impression that the government is about to act on the deep, ingrained institutional racism that holds minorities down. Eliminating the Klan may not do anything about racism except make it less transparent.

This approach of cracking down on Klan crimes to paper over lasting discrimination has rarely been more obvious than during the Reagan Administration. On the one hand, the current Administration has surpassed its predecessors in bringing Klan and other bigoted para-military criminals to the bar of justice. Even beyond that, this President of the United States has visited a Black family whose southern home had been the target of a Klan sneak attack—to demonstrate his personal abhorrence of such violence.

On the other hand, the same Administration has rolled back hard-won, historic victories against racial injustice and dismantled a traditional Federal safety-net to protect poor people. The Administration's financial cutbacks have had devastating effects in the Black ghettos. Unemployment for Black youths soared to about 50%, many dropped out of schools, and the Black prison population has been steadily rising. Cuts in welfare assistance, worsening housing shortages and a growing homeless population have struck ghetto neighborhoods with particular force.

Further, Reagan Administration legal interventions have specifically reversed integration in schools and colleges and in job and promotion affirmative action programs. Black people today face their worst assault not from the hooded men of a violent Klan, but by a Federal government serving as a legal defense committee for White employees or parents claiming "reverse discrimination." The US Attorney-General's office that once slashed away at discrimination in US society, now acts as the chief legal office for reversing the gains of the Civil Rights movement.

It is the President—not just the Klan—who publicly calls "affirmative action" "a kind of reverse discrimination." Unrelenting Federal opposition is destroying more in the Black community (and other poor neighborhoods) than regiments of armed Klansmen ever could. If this destructive warfare was conducted by men waving guns and shouting racist slogans, Whites would be ashamed and the country would be up in arms.

$$* \quad * \quad * \quad * \quad *$$

The Klan has, from its inception, miraculously survived humiliating exposures of its terrorism, corruption and false patriotism. Today's members have a lot to swallow. For example, in 1985, a Klan leader, retired Chief Warrant Officer John A. Walker, Jr., confessed to organizing the most effective espionage ring that ever operated inside the US Navy.

While serving aboard a US Navy Polaris submarine in the 1960s, he and Klan leader Bill Wilkinson, who led the most dangerous US Klan organization, became good friends. After he left the Navy, Walker became Virginia state director of the Wilkinson branch. Wilkinson, who became an FBI informant in 1974, continued his close personal relationship with Walker.

In 1985, Walker admitted being the leader of a family-and-friends espionage network that had fed US national security secrets to the USSR for 19 years. He pleaded guilty to espionage charges, and was sentenced to life in Federal prison.

As 1985 drew to a close, so too did a three month Federal trial in Seattle of Nazis and Klansmen who had organized to overthrow the US government, install White supremacy, and eradicate Jews and racial minorities. Ten defendants were found guilty of using bank and armored car robberies that brought in more than four million dollars, to plot assassinations and a bloody revolution.

Klan members historically have tolerated personally ambitious leaders. Yet citizens still sign up. For members, the hooded order becomes a psychological easy chair, accepting and comfortable. Rather than fault themselves for failures, they are ready to blame "others"—usually the most defenseless citizens, often people in their economic boat. On these neighbors, they heap violent threats and sometimes physical pain. In this way, members do not have to analyze situations and can avoid the pain of guilt.

The hooded order also has served as a powerhouse of explosive activity for those frustrated at their inability to advance. Its activities and structure encourage members, who cannot feel good about themselves or their families, to express a scathing rage toward others. While this detonation may appear to act as an emotional release, it solves nothing more than a moment's need. Psychologically, this violence is a substitute for problem-solving, one that convinces members that they have not sidestepped, but reached solutions.

By venting their frenzy on unprotected, blameless victims, Klan members do not see that they are often as exploited as the minorities they attack. Sadly for all concerned, they besiege and attempt to destroy not an enemy but a potential ally. They have little understanding of a society where there are too few jobs or promotions for Klansmen or their targets. Both are victims.

The Klan member's first problem, then, is personal, since his or her

154

Instructed by experts, Klan children are taught to use firearms. (Stern/Black Star)

actions stem from deep insecurity compounded by ignorance. Successful Klan figures have learned to manipulate that wounded part of a member's psyche and then make it pay dearly for the attention in cash and loyalty.

Periodically, these damaged egos are gathered up and led into bloody battle against some innocent victims. At that point, The Invisible Empire quickly leaps the bounds of a member's psychological problems and shatters the public order and the Constitutional rights of others. The secret order then tests America's patience, Constitution, and justice system.

Throughout its career in the United States, enemies of the Klan have sought to combat it in a variety of ways—both nonviolent and violent. When The Invisible Empire announced a march in Washington, DC, in 1984, for example, the Black community made clear that march would not be tolerated. The demonstration was cancelled. The path of violence, by breaking laws, invites others, such as Klansmen, to break the law.

Some foes of The Invisible Empire have advocated outlawing the organization's violent rhetoric as well as its criminal acts. In an interracial United States, they argued, racist incitements constitute a clear and present danger to communities. But other Klan opponents saw such steps as a violation of the Bill of Rights and insisted that this approach could result in Klansmen gaining publicity, sympathy and new members. The Klan's relation to the Bill of Rights is a question that arouses heated debate.

Throughout its history, and especially recently, those who have opposed The Invisible Empire have devised many feasible, legal approaches. Anti-Klan groups have issued newsletters, and suggested nonviolent anti-Klan techniques.

Civil rights and citizen's organizations have taken the Klan to court for conspiracy, criminal violence and intimidation. The story of Bobby Person who lives in the small rural community of West End, North Carolina, illustrates this approach. Writing in 1985, Person, a guard at a state prison, explained how his personal confrontation with The Invisible Empire started:

> I wanted to advance myself and asked my supervisor for permission to take the sergeant's examination. No black man had ever been sergeant of the prison guard.
>
> I did not know at the time that one of the white guards was a Klansman. That night, a Klan cross was burned in the dirt road in front of my house. My wife and children were terrified. A few nights later, several Klansmen wearing sheets and paramilitary uniforms, and carrying guns, drove up in front of my home and threatened to kill me. My children were so frightened that they did not sleep well for months. Later, shots were fired at the guard tower at night from cars passing on the road.

Person asked for help from the Anti-Klan Network of the Southern Poverty Law Center, and a legal staff came to his aid. The Network brought suit against three Klansmen suspected of these criminal actions and the Carolina Knights of the KKK. Within a few months, a court order halted all Klan military training, and a trial of the three suspected criminals was scheduled. Concluded Person:

Since the Center came to my aid, I have had no problems with the Klan and my family can once again live in peace. . . .For the first time in history, an organization exists that specializes in stopping Klan violence.

Today the Anti-Klan Network unites U.S. citizens against The Invisible Empire. Its lawsuits halted Klan harassment of Vietnamese fishermen in Galveston Bay, Texas; stopped Klan para-military units in North Carolina; and led to ten indictments of Klansmen for beating Black people in Alabama.

To the Anti-Klan network, the secret order has reacted through its legacy of violence. The Invisible Empire leader who was responsible has been sentenced to prison, but other arsonists remain free and have united with neo-Nazi groups.

In October, 1984, FBI officials informed the Center that the Klan planned to assassinate Morris Dees, chief attorney for the Anti-Klan Network. In three months, the Center had to spend $150,000 to protect its employees' lives. A year later law officers secretly recorded a Klan leader saying Morris Dees "gonna end up like Alan Berg." Berg, a Denver talk show host, was assassinated in his driveway.

In 1985, the Anti-Klan Network reported a new, more violent phase in the hooded order's development—that some key Klansmen and Nazis had joined forces to create a dangerous "Underground." This group aims to rule the United States and Canada by overthrowing governments which they claim are under a "Jewish-Communist conspiracy." In 1985, some have been killed in shoot-outs, some jailed and others equally dangerous, remain at large. Reports the Anti-Klan Network:

One consequence already being seen from the decision to form the Underground is that the most extreme and violent radicals from various organizations appear to be entering into greater cooperation.

This new phase is a direct result of an Invisible Empire membership collapse that began in 1983. By 1984, Klan membership had fallen to half of what it had been two years earlier, and entire Klaverns had disappeared. The Invisible Empire rallies brought out far fewer participants and attracted far fewer supporters.

Remaining die-hard members became more desperate for success, and slipped into armed conspiracies against their government. These compact, highly-trained, and heavily-armed units boasted they were prepared, according to their publications, to wage "war against the U.S. government."

In the 1980s, serious problems certainly abound. Adults and children fear an escalating arms race, a widening gulf between rich and poor, diminishing natural resources, toxic waste sites, mounting unemployment, and increased insecurity in old age. Lacking solutions, the KKK brandishes its weapons, shouts its slogans and recruits people who will settle for vulnerable scapegoats.

Children should understand that the affable Klan recruiter in the schoolyard is selling hatred and bloodshed, not a lesson in American civics. Their teachers ought to know that throughout America's growth these hooded people offered not solutions but additional problems. If the program of The Invisible Empire had been successful, the United States would have marched down the genocidal road paved by Adolph Hitler and his Third Reich.

Since the days of Thomas Jefferson, our democratic leaders have warned of the dangers of an uniformed public. Today what is needed is a public informed about how racism and the Klan work. People have to be able to see through its flag-waving, Christian symbolism and catchy phrases to its heritage of discrimination and terror. The hooded order had found fertile soil in ignorance.

Americans who wish to fully understand the reasons behind the Klan's long life should deepen their knowledge of its US legacy. This short volume has only suggested the huge pool of grass-roots, institutional, and high level racism that has nourished The Invisible Empire. It would take many more books to tell so deeply penetrating a story, but that issue is critical in understanding the Klan's role in our society.

Until this nation and its leaders strongly stand against Klan thinking and for equal opportunity, and citizens are prepared to support that view with funds, laws, and educational programs, The Invisible Empire will occasionally flourish. "We've been around a long time," boasted one member in 1985, "and we'll be around." In light of the enduring legacy of The Invisible Empire, this is not an empty boast.

Once citizens were virtually helpless in the face of Klan attacks. Today they can learn about the Klan, and discover organizations that keep one from becoming a helpless victim. The Invisible Empire's history offers some hints:

● Klan leaders use attractively Christian and patriotic, flag-waving propaganda to camouflage their goals of fomenting discord and pulling membership dollars.

● The Invisible Empire has exposed a sad weakness in our society—a willingness by citizens to seek scapegoats among the weakest and least powerful in their communities.

● The KKK has often discovered friends and allies among law-enforcement officials, sometimes high in government structures. This alliance has successfully blocked arrests and convictions in the past.

● Unhappy though the conclusion is, the Klan represents something buried deep in the soul of White society, and the secret order will not depart until that growth is carefully treated by those infected.

● Klansmen are dedicated to furthering their political and other aims through violence, and anyone, not just minorities, can become a Klan target.

Today those who have been victimized by the Klan can turn to the Anti-Klan Network, 400 Washington Street, Montgomery, Alabama 36104. It is only the last link in a chain of resistance to racial injustice that began soon after the hooded order's birth in 1866. The Anti-Klan Network is only one sign that we are not alone.

Thanks to the efforts of women and men who have battled against or exposed the Klan for six generations, the Invisible Empire can no longer attack victims with impunity. Some began their anti-Klan campaigns more than a century ago, others in the 1920s when the KKK soared to popularity, and still others from the 1930s forward. Many risked their lives to bring racial terror to the bar of justice. To the extent that citizens today are free from Klan violence, they are indebted to those brave souls who, often at great cost to themselves and their families, pioneered in an unfinished fight to make this country the home of the brave and land of the free.

ANNOTATED
BIBLIOGRAPHY

*Alexander, Charles C., *The Ku Klux Klan in the Southwest* (Lexington, University of Kentucky Press, 1965) is a scholarly study of a region besieged with Klan activities in the 1920s.

*Chalmers, David M., *Hooded Americanism: The History of the Ku Klux Klan* (New York, New Viewpoints, 1981) is a highly readable, informed history of the Klan between 1915 and the present. Unfortunately, the author's fast-paced style at times treats as farcical antics or unintended humor Klan activities that did not amuse but traumatized victims. The volume has an extensive bibliography of articles on the Klan during all its reincarnations.

*Jackson, Kenneth T., *The Ku Klux Klan in the City, 1915-1930* (New York, Oxford University Press, 1967) focuses on the urban nature and activities of the Ku Klux Klan of the Twenties. It is scholarly and includes a fine essay on source materials.

Kennedy, Stetson, *Southern Exposure* (New York, Doubleday, 1946) is the exciting tale of the first investigative odyssey into Klan ranks after World War II.

National Education Association and The Council on Interracial Books for Children, *Violence, The Ku Klux Klan and the Struggle for Equality* (New York, 1981, Council on Interracial Books for Children). This curriculum guide for teachers is filled with useful printed and visual material for the nation's classrooms on the hooded order and racism in general. It has sections on each of the KKK periods of ascendancy and has utilized documentary materials that are sure to stimulate thinking among students.

Lowe, David., *Ku Klux Klan: The Invisible Empire* (New York, W.W. Norton, 1967) is based on an award-winning TV documentary on the Klan aired in 1965. This is the text and some of the pictures from that documentary.

Sims, Patsy, *The Klan* (New York, Stein and Day, 1978) is a series of interviews with Klansmen, including leaders, who try to justify their organization, perspectives and tactics.

Thompson, Jerry., *My Life in The Klan* (New York, Putnam, 1982). An inside view of the Klan and its activities as seen through the eyes of a reporter who infiltrated it for a year.

*Trelease, Allan W., *White Terror: The Ku Klux Klan Conspiracy and Southern Reconstruction* (New York, Harper and Row, 1971). This heavy scholarly tome focuses on the first Klan during reconstruction and lays bare a record of racial barbarity that had clear political and economic motives and goals.

White, Walter, *A MAN CALLED WHITE* (New York, Arno Press, 1968) is a reprint of the 1948 autobiography of the black man whose light skin enabled him to investigate Klansmen, lynchings and race riots from the inside. White served for three decades as an NAACP leader. His *Rope and Faggot* was also reissued in 1968 by Arno press and is a 1929 study of his anti-lynching investigations for the NAACP.

*These books contain extensive bibligraphies for those wishing to pursue scholarly research.

INDEX

The body of this book was set in
11 point ITC Garamond Light

Book design by Gail M. Peck
Composition by Big E Typographics